Cookbook
by
Wall Drug Gang
200 New Recipes

Compiled by
Friends, Relatives
and Employees

Wall Drug Store
Wall, South Dakota

Printed by
Crescent Publishing, Inc.
Box 98
Hills, Minnesota 56138

THE WALL DRUG STORY

Would you believe it started with the planting of a cottonwood tree in 1906? The town of Wall was established in 1907 and struggled along as a high plains cow town. Ted, Dorothy and Bill Hustead moved to Wall and founded Wall Drug December 31, 1931. It hardly seems possible such an illogical location could be chosen during more trying times than Wall, South Dakota two years after the big market crash.

Dust storms, drought, grasshoppers, crop failures and severe winters added to the miseries of economic disaster in the dirty thirties. Wall was truly the "geographical center of nowhere." But fate hadn't reckoned with the intuitiveness of the Husteads. Dorothy Hustead conceived the idea that many a hot, dusty traveler would welcome a drink of ice water from the Wall Drug well and the first signs popped up on Highway 16. Suddenly, a sleepy little prairie town became the stopping off place for travelers across South Dakota. The Ice Water Store was born.

As the years rolled by, Ted and Bill added attractions to the store for the enjoyment of their customers. The Wall Drug Art Gallery Cafe and the Wall Drug Art Gallery Dining Room have been added where a superb collection of western art is on display. The most recent additions are the new Wall Drug Western Mall, the Rodeo Dining Room and the Wall Drug Emporium. The Western Mall handles everything from post cards to bleached buffalo skulls.

It is impossible to imagine a Wall Drug. But there it is, perched atop the eastern wall of the forbidding Badlands. The hub of a town that has tripled in size and prospered because of its existence. And it all traces back to the ingenuity, generosity and persistence of two people—Ted and Dorothy Hustead.

If one word personifies Wall Drug it would have to be the word FREE!! Ice water, camping guides, Wall Drug signs are free for the asking. Ted Hustead's Cowboy Orchestra, The Chuckwagon Quartet, Six Foot Rabbit, the Buffalo and other points of interest provide free entertainment. And the good old western hospitality—that's not only free, but is a way of life in Wall, South Dakota.

Oh yes! That cottonwood tree planted in 1906 has been completely enveloped by the Wall Drug Cafe. It still thrives and is as much a part of Wall Drug as the Husteads.

TABLE OF CONTENTS

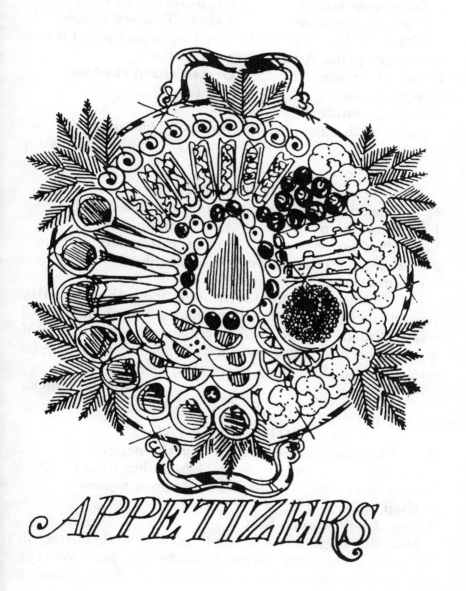

APPETIZERS

AVOCADO DIP

2 avocados
2 Tbsp. sour cream
2 Tbsp. mayonnaise
1 tsp. salt
2 capfuls lemon juice
2 shots Tabasco sauce

Blend all this in a blender until smooth. Spread it out on a large plate. Add a layer each of:

Chopped lettuce
Chopped onion
Chopped tomatoes
Grated sharp cheddar cheese

Serve with nacho or taco flavored Dorito chips.

Wanda Johnston

CHEESE BALL

½ lb. American cheese
1 medium onion
¼ lb. cheddar cheese
3 3-oz. pkgs. Philadelphia cream cheese
½ tsp. garlic salt
½ tsp. onion salt
½ tsp. celery salt
Nuts (optional)

Put first 3 ingredients through food chopper. Mix together with remaining ingredients except nuts until well blended. Divide into 3 balls and roll in nuts if desired. Chill well and serve with crackers. These can be wrapped in plastic wrap and frozen also.

Donna Jedlicka

HOT CHEESE DIP

8 oz. Philadelphia cream cheese
½ c. sour cream
2 Tbsp. milk
1 pkg. dried chipped beef
¼ c. green pepper
2 Tbsp. onion flakes
1 c. chopped pecans
Butter

Mix all ingredients except pecans and butter in casserole dish. Saute pecans in butter and pour over the top of the mixture. Bake uncovered for 30 minutes at 325°.

Mrs. Patrick Rensch

STUFFED MUSHROOMS

12-16 large fresh mush-
rooms
2-3 slices bacon, fried
and crumbled

1 Tbsp. chopped onion
2 Tbsp. grated cheddar
Melted butter

Wash mushrooms and remove stems from caps. Chop the stems and mix with bacon, onion and cheese. Stuff the mushroom caps with the mixture. Brush with melted butter. Broil 7-8 minutes. Serve hot.

Nina Passons

CRAB DIP

2 8-oz. pkgs. cream
cheese
2 6-oz. cans crab
1 clove garlic, minced
2 Tbsp. minced onion

¼ c. mayonnaise
2 tsp. prepared mustard
¼ c. sherry
Paprika

Combine all ingredients except paprika and cook until blended and hot. Transfer to oven-proof dish and reheat when ready to serve. Top with paprika and serve with crackers.

Mrs. Thomas Roe

HOT MEXICANA DIP

1 can condensed bean
with bacon soup
1 6-oz. pkg. garlic fla-
vored cheese food,
diced

1 c. sour cream
¼ tsp. Tabasco sauce
Dash of chili powder
¼ c. minced onion
Corn chips or crackers

Combine soup and cheese in pan; heat slowly, stirring constantly, until cheese melts. Stir in sour cream, onion and Tabasco sauce; heat through. Sprinkle with chili powder and serve hot with chips or crackers.

Sarah Sterritt

DRIED BEEF HORSERADISH BALLS

1 3-oz. pkg. cream cheese, softened

1 Tbsp. prepared horse-radish

Slices of dried beef

Blend cream cheese with horseradish. Spread on dried beef slices; roll up and chill. Cut into bite-size pieces and serve on cocktail picks.

Deane Joyce

EGG JALAPENO CHEESE SAUCE

4 c. shredded cheddar cheese

4 eggs, beaten

1 tsp. minced onion

4 canned jalapeno peppers, seeded and chopped

Combine all ingredients; stir well. Spread mixture into ungreased 8-inch square pan. Bake at 350° for 30 minutes. Cut into 1-inch squares.

Mary Jane Hover

POPCORN PARTY MIX

1 c. corn for popping

¼ c. vegetable oil

¾ c. liquid margarine or butter, melted

¾ tsp. garlic salt

¾ tsp. onion salt

¼ tsp. celery salt

2 Tbsp. Worcestershire sauce

¼ tsp. hot pepper sauce

3 c. pretzels

2 c. salted peanuts

Pop corn in oil. Combine margarine and seasonings. Spread corn, pretzels and nuts in large roasting pan. Pour seasoned margarine over all and toss. Bake in preheated 275° oven for about 30 minutes. When cold, store in tight containers and keep cool. Makes 3 quarts.

Carol Paulsen

Household Hint: Finely grated cheese sprinkled over freshly popcorn makes a suitable tid-bit dish to serve with cocktails.

MOLASSES POPCORN BALLS

1 c. molasses ¼ tsp. soda
½ c. sugar 8 qts. popped corn

(Do not add water.) Boil molasses and sugar until it hardens, not brittle, in water. Add soda the last thing to improve color. Pour syrup over popped corn.

Lucy Hustead

MEXICAN BEAN AND CHEESE PLATE

1-1½ cans refried beans
  (medium size)
½ pkg. Lawry's taco mix
1 Tbsp. bacon grease
½ c. chopped green
  onions
1 green pepper, chopped
1 tomato, chopped
½ can chopped green
  chilies

2 avocados, mashed and
  seasoned with lemon
  juice, salt, pepper and
  Tabasco sauce
½ carton sour cream
1½-2 c. grated Jack and
  cheddar cheese
1 small can whole pitted
  black olives

Heat beans with Lawry's mix and bacon grease, simmer 10 minutes. Spread beans on large platter. Top with other ingredients in order given, ending with olives. Serve with tortilla chips. Double for very large group, using 3 cans beans and 2 platters.

Mary Hustead Bottum

ARTICHOKE HEART DIP

1½ c. mayonnaise
1 small can green chilies,
  diced
Salt and pepper to taste

½ c. diced artichoke hearts
  (in water, not oil)
¼ c. Parmesan cheese

Over a low heat, combine the above ingredients. Make sure not to let it get too hot or the mayonnaise will separate. Use as a dip for chips, crackers, or vegetables.

Jane Rubin

TACO APPETIZER

8 oz. cream cheese,
  softened
1 ripe avocado, peeled
  and mashed

½ c. sour cream
1 Tbsp. lemon juice
1 Tbsp. milk

Blend the above ingredients.

½ c. chopped green
  onions
Shredded lettuce

2-3 chopped tomatoes
8 oz. grated cheese

Spread first mixture on large pie plate or platter. Layer with other ingredients. Serve with Doritos.

Jane Sebade

WATER CHESTNUT APPETIZER

1 lb. bacon, cut slices
  in thirds

2 cans water chestnuts,
  cut in half

Wrap bacon around each ½ chestnut and secure with toothpick. Place in glass cake pan and bake 25 minutes at 350⁰. Drain well, then pour the following sauce over them:

1 c. catsup
Juice of 1 lemon

⅓ c. sugar

Spoon sauce over chestnuts. Let set overnight or all day. Bake at 350⁰ for 30-45 minutes. Serves 6-8.

Bernice Anderson

CHEESE TORTILLA APPETIZERS

6 tortillas
2 c. shredded mild
  cheese

2 Tbsp. seeded and chopped
  canned California green
  chilies or 2 Charingo
  sausages

Put tortillas on a cookie sheet. Top with cheese and chilies. Bake at 425⁰ for 8-10 minutes. Cut like a pizza and serve.

Marcia Sawvell

QUICK HORS D'OUVERES

Cream cheese
Snack crackers

Cocktail sauce
Crab meat

Spread an even layer of cream cheese on snack crackers. Cover evenly with cocktail sauce used for fish, etc. Sprinkle top with crab meat. *Yummy!*

Marsha Sawvell

STUFFED MUSHROOMS

1 pkg. spinach souffle, defrosted
1 c. untoasted bread crumbs
2 tsp. lemon juice
1 tsp. instant minced onions

½ tsp. salt
24 large mushrooms (1½-2 inches in diameter)
Melted butter or margarine
Parmesan cheese

Wash mushrooms, remove stems. In medium bowl, combine spinach souffle, bread crumbs, lemon juice, onions and salt. Place mushrooms on baking tray, brush with melted butter or margarine. Stuff with spinach mixture and sprinkle with cheese. Bake at 375° for 15-18 minutes or 3-4 minutes in microwave.

Evelyn Rush

SPINACH DIP

1 10-oz. pkg. frozen spinach, chopped
1 c. sour cream
1 c. mayonnaise
1 5/8-oz. pkg. Knorr's vegetable soup mix

1 8-oz. can water chestnuts, chopped fine
3 green onions, with tops, chopped fine

Thaw spinach and squeeze dry. Combine with remaining ingredients and chill at least 3 hours.

Ann Rush

FRUIT DIP

1 large carton LaCreme   1 can Eagle Brand milk
  or Cool Whip   ⅓ c. Realemon juice

Mix well and refrigerate. Makes an excellent dip for grapes, peaches, apples, cantaloupe, nectarines, etc.

Betty Bauman

CHEESE SPREAD

1 lb. American cheese   1 egg
1 can evaporated milk

Shred cheese; add milk. Melt over low heat. Add beaten egg and let cook 2 minutes over low heat. Cool and store in refrigerator. Great for stuffing celery sticks—tastes a lot like Cheez Whiz.

Marsha Eisenbraun

CHEESE PUFFS

1 lb. loaf unsliced bread   ½ c. butter
3 oz. cream cheese   2 egg whites, stiffly beaten
¼ lb. sharp cheddar cheese

Trim crust from loaf of bread. Cut into 1-inch cubes. Melt cheeses and butter; remove from heat and beat until smooth. Fold in stiffly beaten egg whites. Dip bread cubes in cheese mixture (be sure they are covered). Place on ungreased cookie sheet. Refrigerate overnight. (Can be frozen.) Bake at 400° for 12-15 minutes until puffy and golden.

Mary Jane Hover

SMOKY BACON CHEESE LOG

8 oz. cream cheese   5 oz. jar sharp cheddar pro-
¼ c. butter   cessed cheese
7 slices crisp bacon   ¼ tsp. liquid smoke
2 tsp. chopped chives

Mix together and form into log. Roll in paprika or dry parsley flakes.

Joan Renner

HORS D'OEUVRES

1 c. mayonnaise
1 c. grated cheddar
  cheese

½ jar black olives, chopped
1 pkg. dried beef, cut up
Rye crisps

Mix first 4 ingredients and put on top of rye crisps. Bake until cheese is melted.

Mary Jane Hover

FRUIT DIP

1 c. sour cream
2 Tbsp. concentrated
  orange juice
1 Tbsp. lemon juice

1 Tbsp. powdered sugar
½ tsp. mustard
¼ tsp. salt

Blend ingredients together. Use as a dip for apples, grapes, bananas, pineapple, melon, plums, etc.

Evelyn Kjerstad

CHEESE BALL WITH EVERYTHING

2 c. shredded Swiss
  cheese
2 c. shredded cheddar
  cheese
1 8-oz. pkg. cream cheese,
  softened
½ c. sour cream
½ c. finely chopped
  onion
1 2-oz. jar pimento, diced

2 Tbsp. sweet pickle relish
10 slices bacon, crisp
  cooked, drained and
  crumbled
½ c. finely chopped pecans
Dash salt and pepper
¼ c. snipped dry parsley
1 Tbsp. poppy seeds
Assorted crackers

Let Swiss and cheddar cheese come to room temperature. In a large bowl, beat cream cheese and sour cream until fluffy. Beat in cheeses, onion, undrained pimento, pickle relish, ½ the bacon, ¼ c. pecans, salt and pepper. Cover and chill until firm. Shape into 1 large or 2 small cheese balls on waxed paper. In a small bowl, combine remaining bacon, pecans, parsley and poppy seeds. Turn mixture out onto clean sheet of waxed paper. Roll ball(s) in seed mixture to coat. Wrap and chill. Let stand at room temperature before serving. Serve with crackers.

Jayme Hustead Chapman

SALMON PARTY BALL

1 1-lb. can red salmon, drained
1 8-oz. pkg. cream cheese, softened
1 Tbsp. lemon juice
2 tsp. grated onion
1 tsp. prepared horseradish
¼ tsp. liquid smoke
¼ tsp. salt
½ c. chopped pecans
3 Tbsp. snipped parsley

Form into ball or loaf. Roll in nuts. Serve with crackers.

Marcia Sawvell

PICKLED VEGETABLE APPETIZER

2 c. cauliflowerettes
2 c. broccoli flowerettes
1 large carrot, cut into 1/8-inch slices
1 celery stalk, cut into 2-inch pieces
1 green pepper, cut into strips
⅓ c. wine vinegar
3 Tbsp. olive oil
1 Tbsp. sugar
1 tsp. salt
1 tsp. Italian seasoning
1 c. pitted ripe olives

Place vegetables on a large platter, arranging it so the largest vegetables are around the outside of the platter and the smaller vegetables are inside. Cover with wrap and microwave on high for 5 minutes. Pour the remaining ingredients over the vegetables and chill for several hours. Drain well before serving. Delicious.

Karen Poppe

SWEET AND SOUR CHICKEN KABOBS

1 deboned chicken breast (about 8 oz.) skinned and cut into 1-inch pieces
1 large green pepper, cut into 1-inch pieces
1 8¼-oz. can chunk pineapple, drained
2 Tbsp. sweet 'n sour sauce

On a toothpick, skewer a piece of chicken, pepper and pineapple. Brush with sweet 'n sour sauce. On a paper towel-lined dish, microwave 15 kabobs, covered with waxed paper, on high for 3 minutes, turning dish once. Repeat with remaining kabobs. Makes 30 appetizers.

Deb Deal

SESAME CHICKEN WINGS

3 c. soy sauce
1 tsp. ground ginger
1 c. packed brown sugar
2 c. wine
3 cloves garlic, crushed

4 dozen chicken wing
drumettes (the meaty
half
1 c. sesame seeds

Combine soy sauce, ginger, brown sugar, wine and garlic in a large saucepan. Bring to a boil, then reduce the heat and simmer for 30 minutes. Add the chicken drumettes and simmer, stirring occasionally, for 15 minutes. Remove the drumettes with a slotted spoon to a rack. Sprinkle with sesame seeds. Place the wings on baking sheets, cover with foil, and refrigerate until 30 minutes before serving time. Preheat the oven to 400º. Bake the drumettes for 15 minutes or until hot and crispy. Serve immediately.

Karen Poppe

APPETIZER MEATBALLS

½ lb. ground round
½ lb. ground sausage
2 c. cubed bread, soaked
in ½ c. milk and
squeezed out
¼ tsp. garlic salt
½ tsp. onion powder

1 Tbsp. soy sauce
½ tsp. Tabasco sauce
½ tsp. M.S.G.
1 can water chestnuts,
minced
1 jar chili sauce

Mix above ingredients except chili sauce. Form into small balls. The secret of cooking these is to place them on a broiler pan. Cook for 10 minutes at 350º. Turn each meatball and cook 10 minutes longer. They don't stick that way. Serve as an appetizer in a chafing dish with chili sauce poured over them. Serve with toothpicks. Makes 45 meatballs.

Mary Hustead Bottum

BREAD & ROLLS

SWEDISH LIMPA BREAD

1½ c. warm water
2 pkgs. active dry yeast
¼ c. molasses
⅓ c. sugar
1 Tbsp. salt

Grated rind of 1-2 oranges
2 Tbsp. soft shortening
2½ c. whole wheat flour
2½-3 c. white flour

Dissolve yeast in water; stir in molasses, sugar, salt and orange rind. Add shortening and whole wheat flour; mix by hand. Add white flour; knead until smooth and elastic. Cover with warm damp cloth; let rise about 2 hours. Punch down; let rise 45 minutes until double in bulk. Form into round loaves. Place on lightly greased baking sheet. Cover with damp cloth. Let rise until double in bulk, about 1 hour. Bake at 375° about 35 minutes.

Ted Hustead's Favorite Brown Bread
by Dorothy Hustead

COFFEE CAKE

1½ c. sugar
2 eggs
½ c. shortening
1 c. milk

3 c. sifted flour
4 tsp. baking powder
1 tsp. salt

Mix together sugar, eggs and shortening. Stir in milk, flour, baking powder and salt. Pour half the batter into a greased 9x13-inch pan.

Streusel Mix:

1 c. brown sugar
4 Tbsp. butter, melted
1 c. nuts

4 Tbsp. flour
4 tsp. cinnamon

Sprinkle half of the streusel mixture over batter. Pour in remaining batter. Top with remaining streusel mixture. Bake at 350° for 30 minutes.

Stella Kleinschmit

CINNAMON SOUR CREAM CAKE

1 c. butter (½ lb.)
1¼ c. sugar
2 eggs
½ pt. (1 c.) sour cream
2 c. flour
½ tsp. soda

1½ tsp. baking powder
1 tsp. vanilla
¾ c. firmly chopped nuts,
  combined with 1 tsp. cinnamon and 2 Tbsp. sugar

In a large bowl of electric mixer, combine butter, sugar and eggs. Beat mixture until light and fluffy. Blend in sour cream. Sift flour; measure and sift with soda and baking powder into the creamed mixture. Add vanilla. Blend well. Spoon half of the mixture (batter) into a 9-inch tube pan which has been buttered and floured. Batter will be thick. Sprinkle half of the cinnamon-nut mixture over batter. Spoon in remaining batter and top with nut mixture. Place in cold oven; set oven to 350°. Bake about 55 minutes. Serve warm or cold. Makes 8-10 servings.

Mary McCullough

QUICK COFFEE CAKE

3 c. flour
⅔ c. sugar
3 tsp. baking powder
½ tsp. salt
½ c. melted fat

2 eggs
1 c. milk
1 can sliced peaches or
  blueberries, drained (or
  1 can applesauce)

Sift dry ingredients; add melted fat, eggs and milk. Mix with fork until moist. Place half of the batter in an 8-inch square pan. Put fruit on top of batter, then remaining batter over fruit.

Topping:

½ c. sugar   4 tsp. cinnamon

Sprinkle fruit with sugar and cinnamon mixture. Bake at 375° for 20-25 minutes.

Mary Jane Hover

19

MYRT'S DATE BREAD

1 c. chopped dates	Pinch of salt
1 c. hot water	1½ c. white flour
¼ c. shortening	½ c. graham flour
¾ c. brown sugar	½ c. walnuts
1 egg	½ tsp. vanilla
1 tsp. soda	

Pour hot water over dates and let stand. Cream shortening and brown sugar; add egg, salt and vanilla. Alternate flours and date mixture, then the nutmeats. Bake in well oiled pan at 350° for 1 hour.

Evelyn Rush

SPEEDY BEER BREAD

3 c. self-rising flour	1 12-oz. can beer (room
3 Tbsp. sugar	temperature)

Place flour and sugar in large bowl; add beer. Mix well and put in greased loaf pan. Bake immediately in preheated 375° oven for 55 minutes. Brush generously with margarine and cool on rack.

Gretta Rensch

DILLY BREAD

1 pkg. yeast	1 Tbsp. butter
¼ c. warm water	2 tsp. dill seed
1 c. cottage cheese,	1 tsp. salt
warmed	¼ tsp. soda
2 Tbsp. sugar	1 unbeaten egg
1 Tbsp. minced onion	2¼-2½ c. flour

Dissolve yeast in ¼ c. warm water; add all ingredients except flour and blend. Add flour; mix well. Let rise until double. Place in 2-quart casserole. Allow to rise. Bake at 350° for 40-50 minutes. Brush top with butter when done.

Ann Rush

JULEKAKE
Norwegian Christmas Cake

¾ c. milk, scalded
¾ c. sugar
½ c. butter
¾ tsp. salt
2 pkgs. active dry yeast
½ c. lukewarm water

4½ c. unsifted all-purpose flour
1 tsp. ground cardamon
½ c. seedless raisins
¾ c. diced citron

Combine scalded milk, sugar, butter and salt in a large bowl and cool to lukewarm. Dissolve yeast in lukewarm water and after a few minutes (about 4), stir into milk mixture. Sift flour and cardamon together and add a little at a time. Mix well after each addition. Turn out on a floured board and knead firmly until smooth and elastic. Turn into a greased bowl; turn over. Let rise, covered, in a warm place for about 1½ hours, or until doubled in bulk. Punch down; turn out onto a floured board. Push raisins and diced citron into dough and knead until well combined. Form dough into two balls. Place several inches apart on a greased cookie sheet. Let rise again, covered, in a warm place until doubled in bulk. Bake in preheated 375° oven about 30 minutes, or until done. Makes 2 loaves.

Dorothy Pagel

BANANA NUT BREAD

2 c. flour
1 tsp. baking powder
½ tsp. soda
1 tsp. salt
½ c. shortening

1 c. sugar
2 well beaten eggs
1 c. mashed bananas
½ c. chopped nuts

Sift together first 4 ingredients. Cream together shortening and sugar. Blend together eggs and bananas. Blend in sifted dry ingredients. Fold in chopped nuts. Bake at 350° for 60-70 minutes. Makes one loaf. I always double the recipe.

Bernice Chapell

APPLE BREAD WITH TOPPING

¾ c. shortening
1½ c. sugar
3 eggs
1½ tsp. soda
3 Tbsp. sour milk
3 c. flour
¾ tsp. salt
1½ tsp. vanilla
3 c. apples

Cream shortening and sugar; add eggs, one at a time. Dissolve soda in sour milk; add to mixture and mix well. Add flour, salt and vanilla; mix in apples. Pour into 2 greased loaf pans.

Topping:

4 Tbsp. butter
4 Tbsp. brown sugar
4 Tbsp. flour
1½ tsp. cinnamon

Combine topping ingredients and spread evenly over batter. Bake at 350° for 1 hour or until done.

Bernice Anderson

ZUCCHINI BREAD

3 eggs, beaten
2 c. sugar
3 tsp. vanilla
1 c. oil
2 c. unpeeled, grated zucchini
3 c. flour
1 tsp. salt
1 tsp. soda
1 Tbsp. cinnamon
¼ tsp. baking powder
Nuts (optional)

Mix eggs, sugar, oil, vanilla and grated zucchini. Sift dry ingredients; add to mixture. Bake in 2 loaf pans at 350° for 45-60 minutes.

Jayme Hustead Chapman
Bernice Anderson

Household Hint: When making muffins or cupcakes use a spring-release ice cream dipper. It will fill the muffin tin ⅔ full without any mess.

FROZEN BREAD CARAMEL ROLLS

2 loaves frozen bread
dough
½ c. butter
1 c. brown sugar

1 6-oz. or 2 3-oz. pkgs.
vanilla pudding
2 Tbsp. milk
½ tsp. cinnamon

Thaw bread dough, but do not let it rise. Grease 9x13-inch pan. Tear one loaf into pieces; drop helter-skelter into pan. Melt butter; add remaining ingredients and beat until smooth. Pour over torn-up loaf. Tear second loaf and throw on top (try to place in empty spots). Let rise 2½-3 hours. Bake at 375° for 30 minutes. Let cool. Turn out on waxed paper.

Frances Dean
Betty Bauman

WHOLE WHEAT ZUCCHINI BREAD

3 eggs
2 c. sugar
⅔ c. vegetable oil
2 c. grated zucchini
1 c. sifted flour
1 c. sifted whole wheat
flour

½ tsp. baking powder
2 tsp. baking soda
2 tsp. cinnamon
1 tsp. salt
2 tsp. vanilla

Beat the eggs until foamy and slowly add sugar. Add vegetable oil and grated zucchini. Set aside. Combine sifted flour and all dry ingredients. Add zucchini mixture to this and then vanilla, walnuts and raisins. Pour into 2 greased and floured loaf pans. Bake 1 hour at 350°.

Jane Rubin

Household Hint: Blend softened butter with honey to use on waffles, pancakes, or homemade bread.

WALL DRUG PECAN ROLLS

1-2 pkgs. yeast (more
    yeast works faster)
3½ c. warm water
⅔ c. sugar
½ c. shortening

2 eggs
1 Tbsp. salt
8-9 c. flour
Oleo, brown sugar and
    cinnamon

Sprinkle yeast on warm water and let bubble about 15 minutes. Add sugar, shortening, eggs, salt and 4 c. flour. Beat on medium speed of electric mixer for 5-7 minutes. Add the remaining flour as needed to knead and make a smooth and elastic dough. You will need most of 9 cups of flour. Let rise until double. Punch down. Let stand 10 minutes. Divide dough in half, roll ½ inch thick. Spread with oleo, brown sugar and cinnamon to cover well. Roll up and slice 1 inch thick. Put in prepared pans—12 to a pan which has been covered with caramel. At this point, you may freeze or bake. Do not preheat oven for frozen rolls. Bake at 300° for 45 minutes until done.

Caramel:

2 c. brown sugar
1 c. oleo

½ c. white Karo syrup
Pecans

Mix in saucepan and heat until dissolved and smooth. Pour into two 9x12x2-inch pans. Sprinkle chopped pecans on bottom of pan.

Elva Hindman

HOBO BREAD

1 c. cooked raisins (re-
    serve 1 c. water
    drained after cooking)
1 c. sugar
3 Tbsp. oil or oleo

2 tsp. soda
2 eggs
2 c. flour
Pinch of salt
½ c. nuts

Cream together sugar and oil. Add unbeaten eggs, flour and salt. Gradually add water to which the soda has been added. Add nuts. Grease and flour three No. 2 cans. Fill cans half full. Bake at 350° for 1 hour. Remove from cans before cool.

Kay Leonard

PARMESAN CHEESE BREAD

1 loaf French bread	½ c. chopped green onion
⅓ c. butter	½ tsp. Worcestershire
1 c. mayonnaise	sauce
½ c. grated Parmesan	Paprika
cheese	

Heat oven to 300°. Cut bread in half lengthwise; spread cut surfaces with butter. Place on ungreased cookie sheet. Bake for 10-15 minutes or until thoroughly heated. Combine remaining ingredients except paprika. Spread over warm bread. Sprinkle with paprika. Broil 3-5 minutes or until light golden brown. Slice and serve.

Suzette H. Kirby

CRANBERRY ORANGE BREAD

2 c. flour	½ c. chopped pecans
¾ c. sugar	1 tsp. grated orange peel
1½ tsp. baking powder	1 beaten egg
1 tsp. salt	¾ c. orange juice
½ tsp. soda	2 Tbsp. salad oil
1 c. cranberries	

Sift together dry ingredients; stir in cranberries, nuts and orange peel. Combine egg, orange juice and salad oil; add to dry ingredients, stirring just until moistened. Bake in greased 9x5x3-inch pan at 350° for 56-60 minutes until done.

Note: 60 minutes is better, and buy good raw pecans.

Mimi Brown

Household Hint: Make a quick breakfast or luncheon treat by topping half grapefruits with crushed strawberries or other berries.

ZUCCHINI COCONUT BREAD

3 eggs
1 c. sugar
1 c. vegetable oil
2 c. flour
¼ tsp. baking powder
1 tsp. soda
1 tsp. salt

1 tsp. cinnamon
1 tsp. vanilla
2 c. grated zucchini
1 c. chopped nuts (optional)*
½ c. raisins (optional)*
½ c. coconut (optional)*

*May use more or less as desired.

Beat eggs, sugar and oil until well moistened. Sift flour, baking powder, soda and salt together. Mix flour mixture with eggs; mix well. Add cinnamon and vanilla; beat well. Add grated zucchini; add chopped nuts, coconut and raisins if desired. Mix. Bake in greased and floured loaf pans at 350° about 1 hour. Yield: 2 loaves.

Optional: Can make a cake with this recipe, just increase sugar to 2 cups with above ingredients.

Marilyn Huether

CHEDDAR CRANBERRY BREAD

3 c. flour
1½ c. sugar
2 Tbsp. vegetable shortening
1½ c. coarsely shredded sharp cheese
1 Tbsp. lemon juice and orange juice and water to equal 1 cup

3 eggs, lightly beaten
1½ c. coarsely chopped cranberries
1½ tsp. baking soda
3 tsp. baking powder
1 Tbsp. grated lemon rind
1 Tbsp. grated orange rind

Sift flour, soda, baking powder and sugar in large bowl. Cut in shortening until crumbly. Stir in lemon and orange rinds and cheese. Add juices and water to well in flour; add eggs. Mix lightly. Add cranberries last. Pour batter into well greased loaf pan. Bake at 400° for 15 minutes and at 350° for 40 minutes longer, until brown. Let bread cool in pan for 10 minutes.

Kelly Engelhart

LEMON BREAD

½ lb. (2 sticks) sweet
  butter
1½ c. granulated sugar
4 eggs, separated
⅔ c. lemon juice
2 Tbsp. grated lemon rind
3 c. cake flour

4 tsp. baking powder
1 c. milk
Pinch of salt
1 c. chopped, shelled black
  walnuts (optional)
¼ c. water

Preheat oven to 350°. Butter two 9x5x3-inch loaf pans with 3 Tbsp. of the butter. In a mixing bowl, cream together remaining butter and 1 c. sugar. Beat in egg yolks, one at a time. Stir in ⅓ c. lemon juice and grated rind. Combine cake flour with baking powder. Add ⅓ of the flour mixture to creamed butter and sugar. Add ½ of the milk, another ⅓ of the flour, remaining milk and remaining flour. Do not overmix. In another bowl, beat egg whites and pinch of salt together until stiff but not dry. Fold beaten egg whites and black walnuts gently into batter. Pour batter into prepared pans. Bake on middle rack of oven for 45-50 minutes, or until a cake tester inserted in center of a loaf comes out clean. Cool bread slightly, remove from pans and cool completely on a rack. Boil remaining ⅓ c. lemon juice, water, and remaining ½ c. sugar together in a small saucepan for 2 minutes. Drizzle the lemon syrup over the tops of the cooled loaves. Let them set until completely cool before wrapping. 2 loaves.

Jayme Hustead Chapman

NUT BREAD

1 c. brown sugar
2 eggs
1 c. sour cream
1 tsp. soda
2 c. flour

Pinch of salt
½ c. walnuts
½ c. chopped maraschino
  cherries

Mix in order given. Bake at 350° in loaf pan. Will make 1 large or 2 medium size pans.

Bernice Anderson

PANCAKES

2 eggs
2 c. sour milk
2 c. flour
2 tsp. baking powder
1 tsp. baking soda
1 tsp. salt
2 Tbsp. bacon fat

Beat eggs; mix with sour milk. Mix until smooth with dry ingredients. Add bacon fat.

Mary Hustead McCullough

AUNT SANDIE'S CINNAMON ROLLS

2 eggs, beaten
4 c. water (130°)
¼ c. sugar
2 tsp. salt
2 Tbsp. oil
⅓ c. powdered milk
10 c. flour (approximately)
2 pkgs. yeast, dissolved in
¼ c. warm water

Mix the first 6 ingredients together. Add approximately 4 c. flour. Mix well. Add dissolve yeast. Add about 6 more cups flour. Knead. Let rise until doubled. Roll out. Spread with oleo or butter. Sprinkle with cinnamon. Roll up and seal. Cut with thread. Make caramel and put in pans. Place the rolls (about 3 dozen) in pans. Bake 20-30 minutes at 350°.

Caramel:
2½ sticks oleo
3 c. brown sugar
10 Tbsp. cream or canned milk
5-6 Tbsp. corn syrup

Melt oleo; remove from heat and add remaining ingredients. Mix.

Jane Sebade

Household Hint: To quickly thaw frozen bread loaves and rolls, place in brown paper bag and put 325° oven for 5 minutes and they will thaw completely.

WHOLE WHEAT ROLLS
WITH CARAMEL TOPPING

2½ c. warm water   5-5½ c. white flour
¾ c. sugar   2 pkgs. yeast
2½ tsp. salt   ¾ c. cooking oil
3 c. whole wheat flour   2 eggs

Put warm water and sugar in a bowl and sprinkle yeast on top. Beat eggs, salt and oil together and add to yeast mixture. Add both flours, mix until smooth and knead. Let rise until double. Punch down. Let rise again and shape into rolls, sprinkling with cinnamon before rolling up.

Caramel:

2¼ c. brown sugar   ¼ c. water
1 c. sweet cream

Mix together. Pour in pan and place rolls on top. Let rise until light and bake for 25 minutes at 350⁰.

Elva Hindman

BUTTERMILK COFFEE CAKE

½ c. shortening   1 tsp. baking powder
1 c. sugar   1 tsp. soda
2 eggs   1 c. buttermilk
2 c. flour   1 tsp. vanilla

Cream together shortening, sugar and eggs. Add flour, baking powder, soda, buttermilk and vanilla. Divide batter in half; spread half into an 8x12-inch cake pan. Sprinkle with half the crumbs. Put on remaining batter and top with remaining crumbs.

Crumbs:

½ c. brown sugar   ½ c. finely chopped nut-
½ c. white sugar   meats
                     1 tsp. cinnamon

Bake at 325⁰ about 35 minutes.

Evelyn Kjerstad

WHOLE HEALTH BRAN MUFFINS

2 c. bran	2 eggs
1 c. whole wheat flour	1 banana
2 tsp. baking powder	2 oranges
2 tsp. cinnamon	1 c. apple juice
1 tsp. nutmeg	½ c. raisins
Dash of salt	½ c. dates

Mix dry ingredients together. Combine remaining ingredients in blender. Mix with dry ingredients. Spoon into muffin cups or greased muffin pan. Bake 25 minutes at 400°. Makes 1 dozen.

Dixie Hustead

SPOON BREAD

2 c. milk	½ tsp. sugar
½ c. cornmeal	2 Tbsp. melted butter
½ tsp. baking powder	3 eggs, separated

Scald milk; add cornmeal and cook until thick. Add salt, baking powder, sugar and butter. Beat egg yolks and add to cornmeal mixture. Beat egg whites to soft peaks and fold into batter. Pour into well buttered 1½-quart casserole and bake uncovered at 375° for 25-30 minutes.

Mimi Brown

FAMOUS SPA MUFFINS

1 c. stone ground whole wheat flour	1 egg
	½ c. honey
1 tsp. baking soda	¾ c. skim milk
1½ c. bran	2 Tbsp. safflower oil
½ c. raisins	

Mix together dry ingredients and raisins. Moisten with egg, honey, milk and oil. Stir only enough to blend. Place one-ounce scoops of the mixture into well greased muffin tins. Bake at 400° for 20-30 minutes. Makes 15.

Marjorie Hustead

ICE BOX MUFFINS

1½ c. sugar
½ c. (heaping) Crisco
1 c. boiling water
1 c. Nabisco 100% Bran
  or Shredded Wheat
2 eggs, beaten

2 c. buttermilk
2½ c. flour, sifted
2½ tsp. soda
½ tsp. salt
2 c. Kellogg's All Bran

Pour boiling water over 100% bran and let stand about 10 minutes. Cream sugar and Crisco; add eggs and buttermilk. Add 100% bran and water mixture. Add flour, soda and salt sifted together; add All-Bran. Mix slightly, do not overmix. Put in covered bowl and refrigerate. Bake at 400° for 10-20 minutes. Keeps for 4 months.

Bernice Anderson

HIGH FIBER-CARROT BRAN MUFFINS

3 c. flour
1 tsp. soda
1½ tsp. baking powder
½ tsp. salt
1 Tbsp. cinnamon
2 c. bran

4 eggs
1½ c. vegetable oil
1¼ c. brown sugar
¼ c. molasses
3 c. finely grated carrots
1 c. raisins

Stir flour, soda, baking powder, salt and cinnamon together. Beat eggs slightly. Add brown sugar, vegetable oil and molasses. Beat well. Add flour mixture with grated carrots. Fold in bran and raisins. Bake in muffin tins at 350° for 25 minutes. These freeze well and are very good. Makes 24 large muffins.

Evelyn Rush

Household Hint: Whip up cheese biscuits with canned dough cut into wedges and rolled in melted butter and grated cheese.

SO GOOD BUNS

2 c. milk
1 stick margarine
1 c. cold water
4 Tbsp. sugar
2 tsp. salt

3 pkgs. dry yeast (Rapid Rise)
2 large eggs
10-11 c. flour

Heat milk with margarine until margarine is melted. Add cold water, then 3 c. flour, sugar, salt and yeast. Beat 4 minutes. Add eggs and beat 2 minutes longer. Add 4 c. flour and beat with wooden spoon. Gradually add another 3-4 c. flour, kneading. The dough is soft but not sticky. Let rise, form into buns and let rise again. Bake at 350° for 20-25 minutes.

Leila Pagel

ONE HOUR DINNER ROLLS ITALIANO

3½-4 c. flour
2 pkgs. yeast
2 Tbsp. sugar
2 tsp. garlic salt
1 tsp. Italian seasoning
1 c. milk

½ c. water
2 Tbsp. butter
1 egg
¾ c. Parmesan cheese
2 Tbsp. melted butter

Combine flour, yeast, sugar, salt and seasoning. Mix well. Heat milk, water and butter until warm (butter need not be melted). Mix at low speed until moistened. Add egg, beat 3 minutes by hand. Stir in ½ c. cheese and enough flour to make firm dough. Knead until smooth and elastic. Place in greased bowl, cover and let rise in warm oven for 15 minutes. Punch down and divide into 15 pieces; form into balls. Dip into the melted butter and then into remaining cheese. Place into well greased 9x13-inch pan. Let rise in warm oven 10 minutes. Bake at 375° for 20-25 minutes until golden brown. Remove from pan and cool.

Pat Cheney

QUICK CHANGE DOUGH

1 c. milk
½ c. sugar
1½ tsp. salt
1 c. cold water
2 pkgs. dry yeast

½ c. warm water
2 eggs
6½ c. flour (may vary—add enough to make soft dough)

Heat milk, sugar, shortening and salt until shortening has melted. Add cold water. Add yeast that has been dissolved in warm water to the cooled mixture. Add beaten eggs. Mix well and add flour, about 2 cups at a time. Mix well. Place in large greased bowl. Cover and store in refrigerator to use later. During refrigeration, the dough rises. To use immediately, let rise in warm place until double in bulk. Use for cloverleaf rolls, coffee cakes, cinnamon or caramel rolls.

Elva Hindman

CINNAMON ROLLS MADE WITH CAKE MIX

3 c. warm water
2 pkgs. yeast
1 pkg. white or yellow cake mix

5½ c. flour (no more)
2 eggs
Brown sugar, cinnamon and nuts

Dissolve yeast in warm water; add cake mix and eggs. Beat well. Add flour and knead until a very soft dough forms. Let rise in greased bowl. Roll out. Spread with oleo, cinnamon, brown sugar and nuts. Roll up like jelly roll. In bottom of pan, put:

1 stick melted oleo
1 c. brown sugar

½ c. canned milk or cream
Nuts

Cut cinnamon rolls and place in pan. Let rise. Bake 30 minutes at 350°. Makes two 9x13-inch pans. Frost with cream cheese frosting if desired or 2 c. brown sugar and ¾ c. cream for caramel (put in bottom of pan before rolls are placed in).

Note: Add enough flour to roll out, but no more than a little hard to handle because it is sticky and soft.

Sylvia Eisenbraun

FRENCH BREAD MONTEREY

1 loaf French bread	½ c. chopped onion (or
Softened butter	1 Tbsp. instant)
1 c. mayonnaise	1 Tbsp. sesame seeds
½ c. grated Parmesan	½ tsp. Worcestershire
cheese	sauce

Cut bread lengthwise in halves, then each half into half crosswise. Spread cut surfaces with butter. Place in oven to heat. Mix remaining ingredients and spread on hot bread. Dust with paprika. Broil slowly until slightly browned. Cut crosswise and serve warm.

Mary Jane Hover

CINNAMON PETAL BISCUITS

2 c. flour	¼ tsp. cream of tartar
3 tsp. baking powder	¾ c. shortening
½ tsp. salt	⅔ c. milk
3 Tbsp. sugar	

Mix as for baking powder biscuits. Roll dough ¼ inch thick.

2 Tbsp. melted butter	1 tsp. cinnamon
⅓ c. sugar	

Brush dough with melted butter. Sprinkle sugar and cinnamon over surface. Cut into eight 12x2-inch strips. Make two stacks of four strips each. Cut each into six 2-inch squares. Place in greased muffin tins, cut side down and press lightly. Bake at 425⁰ for 10-12 minutes.

Venetia Byerly

34

CHOCOLATE CHIP DATE CAKE

1 c. cut up dates
1 tsp. soda
1¼ c. hot water
1 c. sugar
¾ c. shortening

2 eggs
1½ c. flour
2 Tbsp. cocoa
1 tsp. salt

Mix all ingredients together in order given.

Topping:

1 small pkg. chocolate chips

½ c. sugar
½ c. nuts

Sprinkle on top of batter and bake at 350° for 35 minutes.

Donna Jedlicka

CRAZY CAKE

3 c. flour
½ c. cocoa
1 tsp. salt
2 Tbsp. vinegar
1 tsp. vanilla

2 c. sugar
2 tsp. soda
¾ c. salad oil
2 c. lukewarm water

Mix all ingredients together in a large cake pan. Stir with a fork until smooth and creamy. Bake until done at 350° about 35-40 minutes.

Stella Kleinschmit

SOUR CREAM DEVIL'S FOOD CAKE
Makes a large cake!

2 c. sour cream
2 c. white sugar
4 eggs
2 tsp. vanilla
1/8 tsp. salt

2 tsp. soda
3 c. less 2 Tbsp. flour
½ c. cocoa (mix in hot water to make a thin paste)

Combine the first 4 ingredients and mix. Sift together dry ingredients. Add cocoa mixture alternately with flour mixture. Beat well. Bake at 350°.

Bernice Anderson

OATMEAL CAKE

1½ c. boiling water	2 eggs
1 c. quick oatmeal	1⅓ c. sifted flour
1 stick oleo	1 tsp. soda
2 c. brown sugar	¾ tsp. salt

Pour boiling water over quick oatmeal; let stand 20 minutes. Mix oleo, brown sugar, eggs, sifted flour, soda and salt. Beat all together 2-3 minutes. Bake for 40 minutes at 350°.

Frosting:

1 stick oleo	1 c. cocoa
1 c. brown sugar	½ c. nuts
¼ c. cream	

While cake is still hot, mix oleo, cream and sugar; let come to a rolling boil. Then mix coconut and nuts in. Pour over cake and put under broiler to brown.

Donna Stotts

BUNDT CAKE

1¾ c. boiling water	1¾ c. flour
1 c. quick oatmeal	1 tsp. soda
1 c. slightly packed	½ tsp. salt
brown sugar	1 Tbsp. cocoa
1 c. granulated sugar	¾ c. walnuts
1 stick margarine	1 12-oz. pkg. chocolate
2 eggs	chips

Pour boiling water over oatmeal; let stand at room temperature for 10 minutes. Add sugar and margarine; add eggs and mix well. Sift flour with salt, cocoa and soda; add to sugar and mix well. Add ½ of the chocolate chips. Pour into well greased and floured pan. Sprinkle top with walnuts and other ½ of chocolate chips. Bake at 350° for 40-50 minutes.

Margaret Wittmer

RUM CAKE

1 18½-oz. box yellow cake mix	1 pkg. instant vanilla or pistachio pudding
1 c. pecans	½ c. oil
4 eggs	½ c. Bacardi dark rum
½ c. water	

Heat oven to 325°. Grease and flour a 10-inch tube pan. Spread nuts over bottom of pan. Pour batter over nuts. Bake 1 hour and cool.

Glaze:

¼ lb. butter	1 c. sugar
½ c. water	½ c. rum

Prick cake and drizzle glaze over top and sides.

Mrs. C.K. Smith

QUICK SPICE CAKE

⅓ c. shortening	Pinch of salt
1⅓ c. firmly packed brown sugar	2 tsp. baking powder
	¼ tsp. nutmeg
2 eggs	1 tsp. cinnamon
½ c. cold water	¼ tsp. cloves
1¾ c. flour, sifted	1 c. raisins, floured with
⅓ c. nutmeats	1 Tbsp. flour

Sift together flour, salt, baking powder, cinnamon, nutmeg and cloves. Place in large bowl. Add shortening, sugar, eggs and cold water. Beat entire mixture 5 minutes at medium speed. Add nuts and raisins the last minute. Bake 45-50 minutes in medium size cake pan (8x8-inch) at 350°.

Marlene Brown

Household Hint: If you run short one egg for a cake, substitute 1 tsp. cornstarch.

BEER CAKE

⅔ c. shortening	¾ c. buttermilk
2 c. sugar	½ c. maraschino cherry
2 eggs	juice
2 sq. chocolate	4 oz. maraschino cherries,
3 c. flour	chopped
2 tsp. soda	¾ c. chopped walnuts
1 c. beer (no foam)	

Mix in order given. Bake at 350° for 35-45 minutes. Frost with cream cheese frosting.

Frosting:

6 oz. pkg. Philadelphia	1 Tbsp. butter
cream cheese	Powdered sugar

Blend together.

Elsie Fellers

ZUCCHINI CAKE

3 eggs	2 c. flour (may need more if
1 c. oil	zucchini are kind of
3 tsp. vanilla	watery)
2 c. sugar	2 tsp. soda
2 c. shredded unpeeled	¼ tsp. baking powder
zucchini	1 tsp. salt
1 c. raw cranberries,	½ c. pecan meal (optional)
quartered	Dates or raisins (optional)

Combine eggs, oil, vanilla, sugar and zucchini. Then add flour, soda, baking powder, salt and pecan meal; beat well. Stir in cranberries and pour into oiled and floured 9x13-inch pan and bake at 350° for 45 minutes or until tester inserted in center comes out clean.

Cheese Icing:

8 oz. softened cream	1 lb. powdered sugar
cheese	½ c. nuts
1 stick margarine	

Cream together cream cheese and margarine. Work in powdered sugar, beating until light and fluffy. Stir in nuts. (I used salted chopped mixed nuts.)

Mrs. Erhard Eisenbraun

MAHOGANY CAKE

2 c. flour	⅔ c. sour milk
2 c. sugar	2 eggs
½ c. cocoa	½ c. hot water
2 tsp. soda	1 tsp. vanilla
½ c. shortening	1 c. applesauce

Combine all ingredients in order and bake at 350° for 35 minutes. Moist and good.

Olive Humphrey

CARROT-PINEAPPLE CAKE

1½ c. flour	⅔ c. salad oil
1 c. sugar	2 eggs
1 tsp. soda	1 c. shredded carrots
1 tsp. baking powder	½ c. crushed pineapple
1 tsp. cinnamon	with syrup
½ tsp. salt	1 tsp. vanilla

Sift dry ingredients in large mixing bowl. Mix in other ingredients until moistened; beat 2 minutes at medium speed. Bake in greased and floured 9x9x2-inch pan at 350° about 40 minutes. Top with frosting.

Frosting:

3 oz. pkg. cream cheese	¼ tsp. salt
4 Tbsp. butter or mar-garine	2½ c. powdered sugar
	Nutmeats (optional)
1 tsp. vanilla	

Cream together cream cheese and butter or margarine; add vanilla and salt. Gradually add powdered sugar. Top with nutmeats if desired.

Dakota Hildebrandt

Household Hint: Walnut meats will come out whole when the nuts are soaked in salt water overnight before cracking them.

NO FROST CHOCOLATE CHIP CAKE

1 pkg. sour cream choco-
  late cake mix
1½ c. chocolate chips
½ c. oil
4 eggs

1 c. sour cream
1 3-oz. pkg. instant chocolate pudding mix
½ c. warm water

Mix cake and pudding mix, eggs and sour cream. In separate bowl, mix oil, chocolate chips and warm water. Add to cake mix. Bake 45-55 minutes at 350°. May sprinkle with powdered sugar.

Marjorie Hustead

BROWNSTONE FRONT

2 c. flour
1 c. butter
2½ c. sugar
5 whole eggs
2 tsp. vanilla

6 sq. (oz.) baking chocolate
1 tsp. soda
1 tsp. salt
1 tsp. hot water
1 c. buttermilk

Set oven at 350°. Grease two 9-inch cake pans and sift flour. Cream butter and sugar for at least 10 minutes. Add eggs and vanilla. Melt baking chocolate in large double boiler. Dissolve soda and salt in hot water and add to chocolate. Add buttermilk and the chocolate mixture will rise until doubled in volume. Quickly combine chocolate and sugar mixtures and the sifted flour. Bake for 40-50 minutes. Cake is done if it springs back after the center is gently pressed with finger.

Icing:

⅓ c. soft butter
Pinch of salt
1 c. sifted powdered
  sugar
1 egg

3 sq. melted baking chocolate
2-4 Tbsp. milk (enough to
  make smooth spreading
  consistency)

2 c. sifted powdered sugar

Cream first 3 ingredients together until fluffy. Add remaining ingredients. Frost cake. Serve in thin slices. Will serve 20-24.

Mimi Brown

RHUBARB CAKE

2 c. diced rhubarb
1 c. sugar
1 egg
1 c. milk

1 tsp. vinegar
2 Tbsp. oil
1¾ c. flour
1 tsp. soda

Mix all together in order given. Put in 9x13-inch pan.

Grape-nuts   1 c. brown sugar

Combine and crumble over the top. Bake at 350° for 40-45 minutes. Serve with whipped cream or ice cream.

Sylvia Schuler Eisenbraun

APPLESAUCE CAKE

1 c. sugar
½ c. shortening
1 egg
1½ c. unsweetened apple-
sauce
1 c. chopped nuts

1 c. chopped dates
1½ c. raisins (optional)
1 tsp. cinnamon
½ tsp. cloves
2 tsp. (scant) soda
2 c. flour

Mix well and bake 40-50 minutes at 350° or until done.

Bernice Anderson

WILD PLUM CAKE

½ c. oleo
1 c. sugar
2 eggs
½ tsp. salt
5 Tbsp. buttermilk
1½ c. flour
½ tsp. cinnamon

½ tsp. cloves
1 tsp. soda
1 c. wild plums, cooked
and pitted (fill cup with
plum juice)
½ c. nuts

Cream together oleo and sugar; add eggs. Sift together dry ingredients; add alternately to first mixture with buttermilk. Add plums and nuts. Bake at 350° for 25-30 minutes. While warm, top with the following.

Frosting:

¼ c. oleo
3 Tbsp. cream

¾ c. brown sugar
1 c. coconut

Cream together. Cook until sugar is dissolved. Spread evenly over cake. Bake in oven until lightly browned.

Opal Ritzman

CHOCOLATE NUT UPSIDE-DOWN CAKE

10 Tbsp. butter or mar-	2 tsp. baking powder
garine	¼ tsp. salt
¼ c. firmly packed light	1½ c. granulated sugar
brown sugar	2 eggs, separated
⅔ c. light corn syrup	3 sq. unsweetened choco-
¼ c. heavy cream	late, melted
1 c. broken walnuts	1 tsp. vanilla
1¾ c. sifted cake flour	1 c. milk

Melt 4 Tbsp. butter or margarine in a small saucepan; stir in brown sugar and heat until bubbly. Stir in corn syrup and cream; heat, stirring constantly, just to boiling. Add nuts; pour into a generously buttered 10-inch (12-cup) bundt pan (mixture will be thin). Let stand while preparing cake batter.

Sift flour, powder and salt onto waxed paper. Beat remaining butter or margarine until soft in large bowl. Gradually beat in granulated sugar until well combined. Beat in egg yolks, chocolate and vanilla until well combined. Add flour mixture, alternately with milk, beginning and ending with flour. Beat egg whites until stiff in a small bowl; fold into cake batter. Spoon batter evenly over nut mixture in pan. Bake at 350° for 45 minutes or until cake tester inserted in center comes out clean. Loosen cake from edges with a small knife. Cover pan with serving plate; invert; shake gently, then lift off pan. Scoop out any nuts and syrup clinging to pan onto cake with a rubber scraper. Serve with whipped cream.

Jean Hunter

Household Hint: Buy bananas when they are overripe. Mash and measure them into 1 cup units. Place in freezer containers and store in freezer. Thaw when needed for bread and cake.

HUMMINGBIRD CAKE

3 c. all-purpose flour
2 c. sugar
1 tsp. soda
1 tsp. salt
1 tsp. cinnamon
3 eggs, beaten
1 c. vegetable oil
1½ tsp. vanilla extract

1 tsp. butter flavor
1 8-oz. can crushed pine-
  apple, undrained
1 c. chopped pecans
2 c. chopped bananas
Hummingbird Cream
  Cheese Frosting
½ c. chopped pecans

Combine flour, sugar, soda, salt and cinnamon in large mixing bowl. Add eggs and oil, stirring until dry ingredients are moistened. Do not beat. Stir in vanilla extract, butter flavor, pineapple, 1 c. pecans and bananas. Spoon batter into three 9-inch round, greased and floured cake pans. Bake at 350⁰ for 25-30 minutes or until a wooden toothpick inserted in center comes out clean. Cool in pans for 10 minutes, remove from pans and cool completely. Spread frosting between layers and on top and sides of cake; then sprinkle ½ c. chopped pecans on top. Refrigerate. Flavors blend and intensify upon standing for 24 hours after baking. Makes one 3-layer cake.

Hummingbird Cream Cheese Frosting:

1 8-oz. pkg. cream cheese,
  softened
½ c. butter or margarine,
  softened

1 16-oz. pkg. powdered
  sugar, sifted
1 tsp. vanilla-nut extract

Combine cream cheese and butter, beating until smooth. Add powdered sugar and vanilla-nut extract, beat until light and fluffy. Makes enough frosting for one three-layer cake.

Elva Hindman

Household Hint: Use a wet knife to cut a fresh cake.

CHOCOLATE ZUCCHINI CAKE

½ c. butter   2½ c. flour
½ c. oil   ¼ c. cocoa
1¾ c. sugar   1 tsp. soda
2 eggs   1 tsp. salt
2 c. zucchini   ¾ c. chocolate chips
½ c. milk   ¾ c. nuts
1 tsp. vanilla

Cream together first 7 ingredients. Mix together dry ingredients and add to batter. Pour into 9x13-inch pan. Top with chocolate chips and nuts. Bake 60 minutes at 325°.

Sylvia Schuler Eisenbraun

CHOCOLATE FUDGE CAKE

1⅔ c. all-purpose flour   1½ c. buttermilk
1½ c. sugar   ½ c. shortening
⅔ c. cocoa   2 eggs
1½ tsp. soda   1 tsp. vanilla
1 tsp. salt

Grease a 9x13-inch pan. Mix in order given and bake 35-40 minutes at 350°.

Marsha Eisenbraun

NORWEGIAN APPLE CAKE

2 eggs   ½ tsp. salt
1½ c. sugar   2 tsp. baking powder
1 c. flour   2 c. apples

Beat eggs and sugar well. Add flour, salt, baking powder and apples. Bake in a greased 9x12-inch pan at 350° for 35 minutes. Top with whipped cream.

Carol Hammer

CRANBERRY CAKE

¼ c. butter	½ tsp. salt
1 c. sugar	1 c. milk
2 c. flour	1 tsp. vanilla
3 tsp. baking powder	2 c. whole cranberries

Cream butter and sugar. Sift flour, baking powder and salt; add to butter and sugar alternately with milk and vanilla. Add cranberries. Put in 9-inch layer greased cake pan. Bake at 400° for 40 minutes. Serve with Hot Butter Sauce.

Hot Butter Sauce:

½ c. butter, slightly browned	¾ c. light cream
	1 c. sugar

Bring to a boil and serve on Cranberry Cake.

Carla Sahr

SOCK IT TO ME CAKE

Filling:

1 c. chopped nuts	2 tsp. cinnamon
2 Tbsp. brown sugar	

Combine ingredients and set aside.

1 pkg. yellow cake mix	¼ c. sugar
1 c. (8 oz.) dairy sour cream	4 eggs
	¼ c. water
½ c. Crisco oil (other oils may make it fall)	

Blend cake mix, sour cream, oil, sugar, water and eggs at high speed for 2 minutes. Pour ⅔ of the batter into a greased and floured tube pan. Sprinkle the filling over the batter, then pour remaining batter on top. Bake at 375° for 45-55 minutes (until the cake springs back when lightly touched). Cool right side up about 25 minutes, then remove from pan. Requires no frosting.

Elva Hindman

CRUMB CAKE

2 c. flour   1 c. sugar
¾ c. shortening
  Mix the above until crumbly, reserve ¾ cup.
1 egg   1 tsp. baking powder
1 tsp. soda   1 c. light cream
½ tsp. cloves   1 c. nuts
1 tsp. cinnamon
  Mix together. Add crumb mixture (except the reserved ¾ cup). Stir together. Sprinkle reserved crumbs on top of cake before baking. Bake at 350⁰.

Leila Pagel

NEVER FAIL CHOCOLATE FROSTING

½ c. brown sugar   ½ c. chopped nuts
2 Tbsp. butter   ¼ c. water
1 sq. chocolate   1 c. powdered sugar
1/8 tsp. salt   (approx.)
  Blend all ingredients except powdered sugar together. Place over low heat to cook 3 minutes; stir to prevent sticking. Remove from heat and cool slightly. Add powdered sugar to make spreading consistency. Add nuts. Enough for 1 loaf cake or 12 cupcakes.

Olive Humphrey

CHOCOLATE FROSTING

1 c. sugar   2 Tbsp. butter
2 Tbsp. cocoa   1 tsp. vanilla
3 Tbsp. milk   1 egg
  Combine all ingredients and boil just 2 minutes, stirring constantly. Cool to lukewarm. Beat until creamy and it loses its gloss. Spread on cake. This frosting never gets too hard.

Marilyn Drewitz

ANGEL FOOD CAKE TOPPING

4 egg yolks   1 c. sugar
Juice of 2 oranges   1 c. whipped cream
Rind of ½ orange

Cook first 4 ingredients in double boiler until thick. Store in refrigerator until ready to use. Add whipped cream.

Violet Rickard

TOFFEE BARS

½ c. butter or margarine   1 egg yolk
1 c. packed brown sugar   2 large Hershey sweet
2 c. sifted flour   chocolate bars
1 tsp. vanilla   Chopped nuts

Cream butter and sugar; add egg yolk and vanilla. Add flour gradually; mix well. Spread on ungreased cookie sheet, pressing it down evenly. Bake 20 minutes at 350⁰. After 10 minutes of baking, melt Hershey bars in double boiler. Spread on toffee mixture while both are still warm. Sprinkle with nuts and cut into squares. Refrigerate the whole pan for about 30 minutes to harden chocolate. Makes 4-5 dozen.

Mary Hustead Bottum

DATE SQUARES

½ lb. pitted dates   1 c. white sugar
1 c. water

Cook until marmalade consistency. Combine:

1 c. butter or oleo, melted   1½ c. uncooked oatmeal
1¾ c. flour   ½ tsp. soda
1 c. brown sugar   ½ c. chopped walnuts

Mix thoroughly. Divide in half. Put half of the mixture into an 8x10-inch cake pan. Spread date mixture over top. Top with remaining crumbs. Bake 45 minutes at 350⁰. When cool, cut into bars.

Myrtle Paulsen

CARROT BARS

4 eggs
2 c. sugar
1½ c. Crisco oil
2 c. flour
1 tsp. salt

2 tsp. soda
2 tsp. cinnamon
3 small jars carrot baby food

Beat eggs until thick. Add remaining ingredients except carrots. Mix together and add carrots. Grease and flour a 12x15-inch jelly roll pan. Bake 25-30 minutes at 350°.

Icing:
1 stick oleo
2 c. powdered sugar

2 small pkgs. Philadelphia cream cheese

Melt oleo; stir in powdered sugar and cream cheese.

Mrs. Patrick Rensch

BROWNIES

2 sticks oleo
2 c. sugar
1¾ c. flour

6 Tbsp. cocoa
4 eggs
2 tsp. vanilla

Mix together oleo, sugar, flour, cocoa, eggs and vanilla. Bake at 325° for 30 minutes.

Frosting:
2 c. powdered sugar
½ tsp. vanilla
½ stick oleo, melted

3 Tbsp. cocoa
2 Tbsp. strong coffee (or to spreading consistency)

Mix ingredients together and frost cooled brownies.

Betty Morris

Household Hint: If you drop an egg on the floor, sprinkle it heavily with salt and leave it 5-10 minutes. Then sweep the dried egg into a dust pan.

FUDGE BAR

1 c. white sugar	2 c. flour
1 c. brown sugar	1 tsp. soda
1 c. oleo	½ tsp. salt
2 eggs	3 c. uncooked oatmeal

Cream white sugar, brown sugar and oleo; add eggs, flour, soda, salt and oatmeal. Mix well. Grease a 9x13-inch pan. Pat half of mixture into pan. Cover with filling (below); pat remaining mixture on top. Bake at 350° for 25-30 minutes. Cut when cool.

Filling:

1 12-oz. pkg. chocolate chips	1 c. sweetened condensed milk
½ c. oleo	

Stir over low heat until melted.

Margaret Kuntz

COCONUT LEMON SQUARES

1 c. unsifted flour	2 eggs, beaten
2 Tbsp. granulated sugar	1 c. brown sugar
1/8 tsp. salt	1 c. coconut
⅓ c. soft butter or margarine	1 Tbsp. lemon juice
	⅓ c. chopped pecans

Combine flour, sugar and salt; cut in butter until mixture is like coarse meal. Press into an ungreased 8-inch or 9-inch square pan. Bake at 350° for 15 minutes. Mix remaining ingredients. Spread over baked mixture. Bake 30 minutes. Loosen edges while warm. If desired, spread with lemon sugar glaze:

⅔ c. sifted confectioner's sugar	1 Tbsp. lemon juice

Stir lemon juice into confectioner's sugar until smooth.

Mary Hansen

LEMON SQUARES

2 c. flour
1 c. margarine
½ c. powdered sugar
4 eggs

2 c. sugar
6 Tbsp. lemon juice
4 Tbsp. flour
½ tsp. baking powder

Mix first 3 ingredients together. Pat into a greased 9x13-inch pan. Bake 20-25 minutes at 350⁰. Beat eggs slightly. Add remaining ingredients. Spread over top of first mixture and bake 25 minutes more. Sprinkle powdered sugar on top. Cut into squares to serve.

Joyce Keith

BUTTERMILK BROWNIES

1 c. butter or margarine
1 c. water
⅓ c. unsweetened cocoa powder
2 c. all-purpose flour
2 c. sugar

1 tsp. baking soda
½ tsp. salt
2 slightly beaten eggs
½ c. buttermilk
1½ tsp. vanilla

In saucepan, combine butter, water and cocoa. Bring to boiling, stirring constantly. Remove from heat. In large mixing bowl, stir together flour, sugar, soda and salt. Stir in eggs, buttermilk and vanilla. Add cocoa mixture. Mix until blended. Pour into one greased 15x10x1-inch baking pan or two 11x7x1½-inch pans or two 9x9x2-inch pans. Bake at 375⁰ for 20 minutes. Immediately pour Cocoa Buttermilk Frosting over brownies; spread evenly. Cool, cut into bars. Makes 5 dozen bars.

Cocoa Buttermilk Frosting:
¼ c. butter
3 Tbsp. unsweetened cocoa powder
3 Tbsp. buttermilk

2¼ c. sifted powdered sugar
½ c. chopped nuts
½ tsp. vanilla

In saucepan, mix butter, cocoa and buttermilk. Cook and stir to boiling, remove from heat. Beat in powdered sugar, walnuts and vanilla.

Marilyn Huether

51

BROWNIES

2 c. sugar
1½ c. flour
¼ c. oil
4 eggs

1 tsp. salt
2 tsp. vanilla
¼ c. cocoa
Chopped nuts (optional)

Mix all ingredients in a bowl just until thoroughly mixed. Pour into greased and floured 9x13-inch pan. Bake at 350° for 25 minutes.

Gretchen Rausch

PUMPKIN BARS

2 c. sugar
1 c. vegetable oil
2 c. pumpkin
4 eggs
2 tsp. cinnamon

½ tsp. salt
1 tsp. soda
2 tsp. baking powder
2 c. flour

Mix first 4 ingredients. Sift and add remaining ingredients. Pour batter into two 9x13-inch pans. Bake at 350° for 25 minutes.

Frosting:

3 oz. cream cheese
1 tsp. vanilla
¾ stick margarine

1 Tbsp. cream
1¾ c. powdered sugar

Mix together and spread over bars. These bars freeze well.

Marcia Sawvell

RASPBERRY BARS

¾ c. margarine
1 c. packed brown sugar
1½ c. flour
1 tsp. salt

½ tsp. soda
1½ c. oatmeal (raw)
1 10-oz. jar red raspberry
preserves

Cream margarine and sugar; add dry ingredients. Mix well. Press half of the mixture into a greased 9x13-inch pan. Spread with preserves. Sprinkle with remaining crumbs. Bake at 400° for 20-25 minutes. Cool and cut into bars.

Bernice Anderson

APPLE BARS

2½ c. flour   1 egg yolk (add milk to
¾ tsp. salt   measure ⅔ cup)
1 c. oleo

Mix flour, salt and oleo. Add egg yolk and milk; mix well. Roll out half of the mixture and spread in a bar pan.

3 c. sliced apples   2 Tbsp. flour
1⅓ c. sugar   4 Tbsp. tapioca
¼ tsp. cinnamon   2 egg yolks

Mix apples with sugar, cinnamon, flour and tapioca. Cover crust with apple mixture. Top with rest of crust mixture. Beat egg yolks until foamy. Spread on top of the dough. Bake at 425° for 10 minutes and then at 375° for 20 minutes. When cool, you can cut into pieces and freeze if desired. These are really good.

Carol Hammer

SOUR CREAM RAISIN BARS

Crust:
1¾ c. quick cooking   1 tsp. baking soda
  rolled oats   1 c. butter or margarine,
1¾ c. all-purpose flour   softened
1 c. packed brown sugar

Heat oven to 350°. Combine crust ingredients. Reserve 1½ cups for topping. Press remaining mixture on bottom of lightly greased 9x13x2-inch pan. Bake 15 minutes.

Filling:
2 c. raisins   1½ c. sour cream
¼ tsp. salt   3 egg yolks
1 c. sugar   3 Tbsp. cornstarch
1 tsp. cinnamon

Combine filling ingredients in saucepan. Cook over medium heat, stirring constantly until thickened. Pour over baked crust. Top with reserved crumbs. Bake about 20 minutes longer. Cool and cut into bars. Makes 4 dozen 1x2-inch bars.

Gretta Rensch

CHERRY STREUSEL BARS

⅔ c. butter or margarine   2 c. flour
½ c. sugar   1 can cherry pie filling
½ c. coconut or chopped
   nuts (optional)

Cut butter into flour and sugar until particles are fine. Set aside 1 cup. Press remainder into bottom of greased 9x13-inch pan. Bake at 375° for 12-15 minutes or until golden brown. Spoon cherries over partially baked crust. Combine coconut with reserved flour mixture. Sprinkle over cherries. Bake 25-30 minutes or until light golden brown. I have used both peach and blueberry pie filling and they are very good also.

Marsha Eisenbraun

CHUCKIE'S OATMEAL COOKIES

1 c. raisins   2 c. flour
1 c. sugar   1 tsp. soda
1 c. shortening (part   1 tsp. baking powder
   butter for flavor)   ½ tsp. cinnamon
2 eggs, beaten   ½ tsp. nutmeg
1 c. oatmeal   ½ c. nuts

Cook raisins until tender and set aside (reserve water). Blend sugar and shortening; add beaten eggs and then oatmeal. Sift together and add flour, soda, baking powder, cinnamon and nutmeg. Add cooked raisins and 5 Tbsp. of their juice, along with the nutmeats. Chill batter before dropping from a teaspoon onto a lightly greased cookie sheet. Bake at 375° about 15 minutes, or until light brown.

Charles and Esther Hustead

Household Hint: To speed ripening of unripe fruit, place in a brown bag.

PEANUT BUTTER COOKIES

1½ c. flour
¾ tsp. soda
1½ tsp. baking powder
½ c. peanut butter
¼ tsp. salt

½ c. granulated sugar
½ c. firmly packed brown sugar
3 well beaten eggs

Sift flour; sift again with soda, baking powder and salt. Soften peanut butter in mixing bowl and cream with sugar. Add well beaten eggs and flour mixture. Stir until well mixed. Drop ½-inch balls of dough on cookie sheet 1½ inches apart. Flatten with fork which has been dipped in flour, making criss-cross pattern. Bake at 350° about 10 minutes.

Olive Humphrey

POWDERED SUGAR COOKIES

1 c. powdered sugar
1 c. butter
1 egg
½ tsp. soda

½ tsp. cream of tartar
½ tsp. salt
1 tsp. vanilla
2 c. flour

Cream sugar and butter; add egg, vanilla and sifted dry ingredients. Roll into balls and press on cookie sheet with glass dipped in granulated sugar. Or dough can be rolled out on floured surface and cut with cookie cutters.

Sheila Gottron

THREE-IN-ONE COOKIES

1 c. shortening, softened
1 c. granulated sugar
1 c. brown sugar
2 eggs
½ tsp. vanilla
1¼ c. sifted flour

1 tsp. soda
½ tsp. salt
3 c. oatmeal
1 c. coconut
1 c. chocolate chips

Beat shortening, sugar, eggs and vanilla until creamy. Add flour, soda and salt; blend well. Stir in oatmeal, coconut and chocolate chips. Drop by teaspoonfuls. Bake at 350°.

Delores Eisenbraun

RAISIN DROP COOKIES

2 c. raisins	2 c. white sugar
1 c. water	1 c. shortening
1 tsp. baking powder	½ tsp. salt
1 tsp. vanilla	¼ tsp. nutmeg
3 eggs, well beaten	1 tsp. cinnamon
4 c. flour	1 c. walnuts
1 tsp. soda	

Boil water and raisins briskly for 5 minutes. Cool. Stir in soda and let stand. Cream shortening and sugar. Add vanilla, eggs and cooled raisins with liquid. Add sifted dry ingredients. Stir in nuts. Drop onto greased cookie sheets. Bake at 425° for 10-15 minutes.

Bernice Anderson

PEBERNODDER
(Peppernuts)

1 c. sugar	1½ tsp. ginger
5 Tbsp. water	½ c. butter
2½ Tbsp. dark corn	1½ tsp. baking soda
syrup	3 Tbsp. cognac
2 tsp. cinnamon	3-4 c. all-purpose flour
1 tsp. cloves	

Combine sugar, water, corn syrup, cinnamon, cloves and ginger. Heat through, but do not boil. Remove from heat and stir in butter. Stir until mixture is cool. Add baking soda, cognac and enough flour to make a stiff dough. Let dough stand at room temperature for 35 to 48 hours. Knead again. Roll out as thin as possible. Snip off small pieces of dough and roll into walnut-size balls. Bake on greased cookie sheets at 375° about 10 minutes.

Dorothy Pagel

Household Hint: Add dry pudding mix to your cookie recipes. This makes a cookie that is more moist.

RAISIN CRISPIES COOKIES

¾ c. seedless raisins   ¾ c. sifted flour
½ c. shortening   ½ tsp. salt
¼ c. water   ½ tsp. soda
1 tsp. vanilla extract   ½ tsp. cinnamon
1 c. packed brown sugar   1½ c. rolled oats

Rinse and drain raisins. Combine with shortening and water. Heat only until shortening melts, stirring constantly. Cool. Stir in vanilla and sugar. Sift flour with salt, soda and cinnamon. Blend into first mixture. Stir in oats. Drop by teaspoonfuls onto greased cookie sheet. Bake at 350° about 10 minutes. Cool a minute or two, then remove to wire rack to cool. Makes about 3½ dozen crisp wafers.

Cecilia Melvin

CHOCOLATE COOKIES

1 c. sugar   ¼ tsp. salt
1¾ c. flour   ½ c. shortening
¼ c. cocoa   ¼ c. buttermilk
1½ tsp. baking powder   1 egg
¼ tsp. soda   1 tsp. vanilla

Mix thoroughly. Drop by teaspoonfuls onto cookie sheet. Press down with glass dipped in water, then sugar. Put walnut in center of cookie. Bake at 360° about 10 minutes.

Mary Hansen

SOUR CREAM WHITE COOKIES

2 c. sugar   2 tsp. soda
1 c. butter   1 tsp. nutmeg or vanilla
1 c. country sour cream   Flour to roll
4 eggs

Cream butter and sugar together. Beat eggs; stir well. Add sour cream with soda in; add flavoring. Add enough flour just to roll. Sprinkle with sugar. Cut with cookie cutter. Bake until slightly browned, 10-12 minutes.

Violet Rickard

COCONUT CORN FLAKE MACAROONS

2 egg whites	¾ c. sugar
Pinch of salt	2½ c. corn flakes
1/8 tsp. cream of tartar	1 c. shredded coconut
1 tsp. vanilla	½ c. chopped walnuts

Beat egg whites until frothy; add salt and cream of tartar. Gradually add sugar, beating until stiff, but not dry. Add vanilla. Carefully fold in corn flakes, coconut and nuts. Drop by teaspoonfuls onto well buttered baking sheet. Bake at 300° until firm and just delicately browned, 20-25 minutes.

Marjorie Bielmaier

DATE DROPS

1 c. chopped dates	1½ c. flour
½ c. water	½ tsp. salt
1 egg	½ tsp. baking powder
½ c. brown sugar	¼ tsp. soda
½ c. margarine	½ c. chopped nuts (pecans
¼ c. milk	are best)

Bring dates and water to a boil. Simmer 5 minutes and let cool. Set aside 2 Tbsp. of mix for frosting. To remaining mixture, beat in egg, sugar, margarine and milk. Sift dry ingredients and add to egg mixture; stir in nuts. Drop by teaspoonfuls onto ungreased baking sheet. Bake 10-12 minutes at 375°. When cool, frost with:

Date Frosting:

3 Tbsp. soft margarine	½ tsp. vanilla
1½ c. powdered sugar	2 Tbsp. date mix (reserved)

Add enough milk to make it of spreading consistency.

Venetia Byerly

Household Hint: A frozen egg can be made as good as before by placing it in a cup of boiling water for a few minutes.

FILLED DATE COOKIES

Filling:

1 pkg. dates	1 c. sugar (white or brown)
½ tsp. vanilla	1 c. water

Cook until thick. Let cool.

Crust:

1 c. melted butter	1 c. brown sugar
1½ c. oatmeal	1½ c. flour
½ tsp. soda	½ tsp. salt
1 c. chopped nuts	

Mix together. Put half of mixture in pan. Add filling and place remaining half of mixture on top. Bake 20 minutes.

Violet Rickard

SUGAR COOKIES

1 c. butter	2½ c. sifted flour
1 c. sugar	½ tsp. soda
1 tsp. vanilla	¾ tsp. salt
1 egg	2 Tbsp. milk

Cream together first 4 ingredients. Stir in dry ingredients. Blend in milk. Dip balls of dough into sugar and press down dough with glass bottom. Bake at 400° for 10 minutes.

Connie Rensch

PUMPKIN COOKIES

1 c. butter	1 tsp. baking powder
1 c. sugar	1 tsp. soda
1 c. pumpkin	1 tsp. cinnamon
1 egg	½ tsp. salt
1 tsp. vanilla	½ c. dates, raisins or nuts
2 c. flour	

Stir butter until creamy. Work in sugar until smooth. Add pumpkin, egg and vanilla; beat well. Sift together dry ingredients. Blend into creamed mixture. Add dates, raisins or nuts. Drop by spoonfuls onto a greased cookie sheet. Bake at 375° for 10-15 minutes.

Mary Helen Peterson

OATMEAL COOKIES

4 c. old-fashioned oats   ¾ c. oil
2 c. packed brown sugar
Mix well and let set on counter overnight.
2 beaten eggs   Pinch of salt
2 tsp. vanilla
Add to first mixture. Mix well. Drop onto greased cookie sheet and bake at 350° for 8-10 minutes. (When you put these on the cookie sheet, peak them up. Let them cool before removing from cookie sheet.) Makes about 60 cookies.

Nyla Ghering

ORANGE GINGER COOKIES

1 c. butter or margarine   2 tsp. soda
1½ c. sugar   2 tsp. cinnamon
1 egg   2 tsp. ginger
2 Tbsp. light corn syrup   ½ tsp. cloves
3 c. sifted all-purpose   1 Tbsp. shredded orange
   flour   peel
Thoroughly cream together butter and sugar. Add egg and syrup; beat well. Sift together dry ingredients; mix into creamed mixture along with orange peel. Shape into two 9-inch rolls about 2 inches across. Wrap in waxed paper; chill several hours or overnight. Slice about 1/8 inch thick. Place 2 inches apart on ungreased baking sheet. Bake at 400° for 5-6 minutes or until done. Makes about 8 dozen.

Mimi Brown

MERINGUE COOKIES

3 egg whites   1 c. sugar
¼ tsp. cream of tartar
Beat egg whites and cream of tartar until stiff. Slowly add sugar. Drop onto brown paper on cookie sheet. Put in 400° oven. Turn oven off and go to bed. They will be ready in the morning!

Marcia Sawvell

CHOCOLATE CRISPY COOKIES

2½ c. unsifted all-purpose flour
1 tsp. baking soda
½ tsp. salt
1 c. margarine, softened
2 c. sugar
2 eggs
2 tsp. vanilla flavoring
4 c. Kellogg's Rice Krispies
1 12-oz. pkg. (2 c.) chocolate morsels

Preheat oven to 350°. Stir together flour, soda and salt; set aside. Beat margarine and sugar until smooth. Beat in eggs and vanilla; mix in flour mixture. Stir in cereal and chocolate morsels. Drop by level tablespoonfuls onto a greased baking sheet. Bake at 350° about 10 minutes or until lightly browned. Remove from baking sheet. Yield: 7 dozen 2½-inch cookies.

Marilyn Drewitz

ONE MINUTE COOKIES

2 c. sugar
½ c. cocoa
½ c. milk
1 stick margarine
2 c. quick oatmeal
½ c. coconut
½ c. peanut butter
1 tsp. vanilla

Mix sugar, cocoa, milk and margarine. Boil for 1 minute after mixture begins to boil. Mix with remaining ingredients. Let stand 5 minutes, then drop onto waxed paper by teaspoonfuls.

Jean Hunter

GINGER COOKIES

¾ c. shortening
1 c. sugar
1 egg
4 tsp. molasses (I use less)
2 c. flour
2 tsp. soda
1 tsp. cinnamon
½ tsp. cloves
1 tsp. (rounded) ginger

Cream shortening and sugar; add egg and molasses. Mix well. Add the soda and spices to the flour, then add to the first mixture. Form into balls and roll in sugar. Bake at 350°.

Bernice Anderson

EASY COOKIES

1 c. sugar   ½ c. canned milk
1 c. peanut butter   5 c. corn flakes
   Mix together and drop onto cookie sheet. Bake at 350°
for 10 minutes.

Nyla Ghering

BANANA OATMEAL COOKIES

1½ c. flour   ¾ c. shortening
1 c. sugar   1 egg
½ tsp. baking soda   1 c. mashed ripe bananas
1 tsp. salt   1¾ c. quick cooking oat-
¼ tsp. nutmeg   meal
¾ tsp. cinnamon   ½ c. chopped nuts
   Cream shortening and sugar; add eggs and beat. Add
remaining ingredients except oatmeal and mix well. Add
oatmeal. Mix and drop by teaspoonfuls onto cookie
sheet. Bake at 350° until done, about 15 minutes.

Evelyn Kjerstad

FAMOUS SECRET CHOCOLATE CHIP COOKIES

2 c. butter   1 tsp. salt
2 c. sugar   2 tsp. baking powder
2 c. brown sugar   2 tsp. soda
4 eggs   4 c. flour
2 tsp. vanilla   1 24-oz. bag chocolate chips
5 c. oatmeal (measure   1 8-oz. plain Hershey bar,
   out and grind in   chopped
   blender)   3 c. chopped nuts
   Cream first 5 ingredients. In separate bowl, blend
oatmeal, salt, baking powder, soda and flour. Mix with
creamed mixture. Add chips, Hershey bar and chopped
nuts. Place golf ball-sized cookies 2 inches apart on
ungreased cookie sheet. Bake at 375° for 6 minutes.
Makes 112.

Sheila Gottron

HUSTEAD'S CHRISTMAS PECAN SNOWBALL

1 c. real butter   2 c. cake flour

4 Tbsp. sugar   2 c. ground pecans

2 tsp. vanilla

Cream butter, sugar and vanilla. Add pecans and flour. Roll into balls or crescents with your hands and barely flatten on cookie sheet. If cookie dough has been refrigerated for a half hour, the balls are easier to form. Bake at 300° about 45 minutes. While still warm, roll in powdered sugar. Store in covered cookie tin.

Kelly Hustead Engelhart

Desserts

RASPBERRY CHEESE CAKE

½ lb. graham crackers,
  rolled fine
2 Tbsp. sugar

1½ tsp. cinnamon
¼ lb. margarine

Mix above ingredients. Press into a 9x13-inch pan.

3 8-oz. pkgs. cream
  cheese
1 c. sugar

3 eggs (beat in one at a
  time)
½ tsp. vanilla

Pour over cracker mixture and bake at 375° for 20 minutes (no longer).

Topping:

2 pkgs. frozen raspberries   2 Tbsp. cornstarch
  (reserve juice)

Thicken raspberry juice with cornstarch. Cool and add the raspberries. Pour over cooled cheesecake.

Leone Huebl

DELICIOUS CHOCOLATE DESSERT

Crust:

1½ c. sifted flour   ⅔ c. pecans
1½ sticks oleo

Mix thoroughly. Spread in a greased 9x13-inch pan. Bake 30 minutes.

Filling:

8 oz. cream cheese
1 c. powdered sugar
1 large carton Cool Whip

2 small boxes instant
  chocolate pudding
3 c. milk

Beat together cream cheese, powdered sugar and ½ carton Cool Whip (use a spoon dipped in hot water as it will be stiff). Spread over crust. Mix chocolate pudding with milk. Spread over cream cheese mixture. Refrigerate for 15 minutes. Cover with remaining Cool Whip.

Dorothy Hustead

MERINGUE SHELLS

4 egg whites   Flavoring to taste
1 c. sugar

Beat egg whites until stiff. Add ⅔ c. sugar; beat. Fold in remaining sugar and flavoring to taste. Cover pan with white paper. Drop mixture onto paper, placing far apart. Bake 1 hour at 250⁰. Let stand in oven (turned off) to dry out. Serve with fruit and cover with whipped cream. Makes 10.

Diane Klein

RHUBARB STREUSEL DESSERT

½ c. sugar   ½ tsp. salt
2 Tbsp. butter   1 tsp. baking powder
6 Tbsp. milk   3½ c. diced rhubarb
1 egg   1 box strawberry Jello
1½ c. flour

Beat together first 4 ingredients. Sift together flour, salt and baking powder. Add to first mixture. Spread into 9x13-inch pan. Put rhubarb on top of batter. Sprinkle Jello over rhubarb.

Streusel:

1⅓ c. flour   Pinch of salt
1 c. sugar   ¼ tsp. cinnamon
¼ c. butter

Mix ingredients for streusel. Sprinkle over rhubarb. Bake 35-40 minutes at 350⁰.

Joyce Keith

FRENCH MINT DESSERT

Vanilla wafers   4 sq. melted semi-sweet
1 c. butter   chocolate
2 c. powdered sugar   2 tsp. vanilla
4 eggs   1 tsp. peppermint

Line pan with vanilla wafers. Beat butter and sugar together. Add remaining ingredients. Beat a full 10 minutes. Place mixture over wafers. Freeze and serve.

Pamela Brekhus McKenney

FRESH PEACH CRISP DESSERT

⅔ c. crushed corn flakes
5 ripe peaches, peeled
  and sliced
2 Tbsp. granulated sugar
⅓ c. orange juice

3 Tbsp. butter
⅓ c. packed brown sugar
½ c. flour, sifted
½ tsp. cinnamon
½ tsp. salt

Line bottom of a greased 9x9x2-inch pan with sliced peaches (layer should be about 1 inch thick). Combine granulated sugar and orange juice; pour over peaches. Cream butter with brown sugar. Sift flour, then measure. Mix and sift flour, cinnamon and salt together. Combine crushed corn flakes with flour mixture. Mix sugar and flour mixture together until crumbly. Spread on top of peaches. Bake at 350° in preheated oven about 25 minutes. Serve hot, topped with cream.

Cecilia Melvin

CHERRY-O-CREAM CHEESECAKE

Crust:

1½ c. crushed graham
  crackers

¼ c. sugar
⅓ c. melted oleo

Prepare graham cracker crust and press into 9x9-inch pan.

1 8-oz. pkg. cream cheese
1 15-oz. can sweetened
  condensed milk

⅓ c. lemon juice
1 tsp. vanilla
1 can cherry pie filling

Let cream cheese soften to room temperature. Whip until fluffy. Gradually add condensed milk; continue beating until well blended. Add lemon juice and vanilla, blending well. Pour into prepared crust. Chill 2-3 hours before putting cherry pie filling over top of filling.

Clarame White

Household Hint: For highest meringues, start with room temperature egg whites.

BAKED GOOD APPLE PUDDING

1 Tbsp. (rounded) flour	Pinch of salt
4 c. sliced apples	¾ c. oatmeal
1 c. sugar	¾ c. flour
1 tsp. cinnamon	½ tsp. baking powder
¾ c. brown sugar	½ c. melted shortening
½ tsp. soda	1 c. water

Mix first 5 ingredients; stir well and pour into greased pan. Combine remaining ingredients except water. Mix well with hands and crumble over apples. Pour water over all. Bake until apples are done at 350⁰.

Myrtle Weifenbach

INDIAN PUDDING

¼ c. corn meal	½ tsp. ginger
2 c. hot milk	½ tsp. cinnamon
¼ c. sugar	¼ c. light mild molasses
1/8 tsp. baking soda	1 c. cold milk
½ tsp. salt	

Gradually stir corn meal into hot milk. Cook over low heat 15 minutes, stirring constantly. Remove from heat. Blend sugar, soda, salt and spices; stir into cooked mixture. Add molasses and cold milk; mix well. Pour into 1-quart casserole. Bake in preheated 275⁰ oven for 2 hours. Serve warm with whipped cream or ice cream, sprinkled with nutmeg.

Marjorie Brown

EASY HOMEMADE ICE CREAM

4 eggs	1 c. sugar
½ tsp. salt	2 boxes instant pudding
1 tsp. vanilla	½ gal. milk (or to fill
1 can evaporated milk	freezer ⅔-¾ full)

Mix first 6 ingredients. Put into an ice cream freezer. Add milk. Crank until ready.

Peggy Harner

CHERRY TARTE DESSERT

1 can pitted pie cherries	1 egg
1 c. flour	½ c. chopped nuts
1¼ c. sugar	1 Tbsp. melted butter
1 tsp. soda	1 tsp. cinnamon

Sift flour, sugar and cinnamon. Add drained cherries and mix well. Add egg, nuts and melted butter. Bake in an 8x8-inch pan for 40 minutes at 350⁰. Serve warm. This can be made while preparing dinner. Cut into 8 squares and serve with hot cherry sauce made of:

Juice from cherries	Dash of cinnamon
½ c. sugar	A little butter
2 Tbsp. flour	Lemon juice

Cook until as thick as you like sauce.

Marie Dartt

BANANA SPLIT

3 sticks butter	Fresh strawberries or
2 c. graham cracker	cherries
crumbs	1 No. 2 can crushed pine-
2 eggs	apple
1 lb. box powdered sugar	1 large carton Cool Whip
5 bananas	1 c. chopped pecans

In a 9x13-inch pan, mix 1 stick butter with graham cracker crumbs. Beat eggs, 2 sticks butter and powdered sugar at high speed of mixer for 15 minutes. Pour into pan. Slice bananas; layer in pan. Add crushed drained pineapple, Cool Whip and chopped pecans in order given. Top with fresh strawberries or cherries. Chill at least 2 hours before serving.

Gayle Eisenbraun

Household Hint: As soon as cake pans are taken from the oven set them on a damp towel to cool for 10 minutes and the layers will slip out.

BROWNIE SHORTCAKE

2 c. sugar
2 c. sifted flour
1 stick oleo

1 c. water
3½ Tbsp. cocoa
½ c. Crisco

Mix sugar and sifted flour in bowl. In pan, let oleo, water, cocoa and Crisco come to a boil. Pour over sugar and flour; beat well. Add:

½ c. buttermilk or sour
milk
2 unbeaten eggs

1 tsp. soda
1 tsp. vanilla

Beat well. Bake at 375⁰ for 20-25 minutes in large cookie sheet (11x16-inch) with sides. While this is baking, mix:

1 lb. (2 c.) powdered
sugar
6-8 Tbsp. milk

1 c. chopped walnuts
3½ Tbsp. cocoa
1 tsp. vanilla

Spread frosting over brownies as soon as removing from oven.

Mrs. Andy Eisenbraun

RHUBARB CRUNCH

1 c. flour
¾ c. regular or quick
cooking oatmeal
1 c. brown sugar
½ c. butter, melted
1 tsp. cinnamon

4 c. diced rhubarb
1 c. sugar
2 Tbsp. cornstarch
1 c. water
1 tsp. vanilla

Mix first 5 ingredients until crumbly. Press half of this mixture into a greased 9x9-inch baking pan. Add rhubarb. Combine sugar, cornstarch and water; cook over low heat until clear and thick. Stir in vanilla. Pour over rhubarb. Top with remaining crumbs. Bake in preheated 350⁰ oven for 1 hour. Serve warm with whipped cream.

Dorothy Hamann

STRAWBERRY CREAM SQUARES

2 3-oz. pkgs. strawberry Jello
2 c. boiling water
2 10-oz. pkgs. frozen strawberries

1 13½-oz. can crushed pineapple
2 bananas, finely diced
1½ c. sour cream

Dissolve Jello in boiling water; add frozen strawberries. Stir until thawed. Add pineapple and bananas. Pour half in 8x8x2-inch pan. Chill until firm. Spread evenly with sour cream. Pour remaining gelatin on top.

Elsie Feller

FANCY ENGLISH TRIFLE

1 qt. strawberries, hulled
1 qt. blueberries (if available), mixed with strawberries)
2 pkgs. frozen raspberries
2 Tbsp. powdered sugar
2 c. milk
2 c. sour cream

2 3¾-oz. pkgs. vanilla instant pudding mix
2 pkgs. frozen Sarah Lee pound cake
½ c. sherry
1 c. heavy cream
2 Tbsp. powdered sugar
¼ c. toasted slivered almonds

Slice strawberries. Mix with blueberries (if available) and 2 Tbsp. powdered sugar. Thaw raspberries. Mix together milk, sour cream and pudding. Slice pound cake into ¼-inch slices. Position slices in bottom of a 3-quart (or larger) clear glass bowl. Drizzle with some of the sherry. All pieces should be touched by the sherry. Cover with ⅓ of the pudding and then ½ of the strawberry-blueberry mixture. Repeat layers using all of the raspberries for middle layer. Repeat layers again using remaining strawberries. Combine cream with sugar. Beat. Decorate surface of trifle with whipped cream. Sprinkle with toasted almonds. Serves 12.

Suzette H. Kirby

APPLE CRUMBLE

6 apples
¼ c. water
2 Tbsp. lemon juice
½ c. sugar mixed with
   ½ tsp. cinnamon

¾ c. flour
½ c. brown sugar
¼ tsp. salt
6 Tbsp. margarine

Pare and slice apples into shallow baking pan. Add water and lemon juice. Sprinkle with sugar mixed with cinnamon. Blend together flour, brown sugar and salt. Work in margarine with a fork until crumbly mixture. Spread over apples in pan and pat smooth with back of spoon. Bake at 375° about 40 minutes. Serve warm with plain cream or whipped cream or vanilla ice cream.

Mary Helen Hustead Peterson

MACARONI DESSERT

1 4-oz. pkg. macaroni rings
1 pkg. lemon pudding
1 egg
1 c. cream, whipped*

2 c. miniature marsh-mallows
1½ c. crushed pineapple, drained

*Or substitute with 1 pkg. prepared Dream Whip.

Cook macaroni rings; rinse and cool. Cook lemon pudding with egg according to directions; let cool. Gently mix all ingredients together. (Can use other fruit in place of pineapple). Serves 10-12.

Helen Eisenbraun

RHUBARB DESSERT

3 c. diced rhubarb
1 c. water
1 c. small marshmallows
1 3-oz. pkg. strawberry Jello

1 c. sugar
1 8-oz. carton whipped topping

Boil rhubarb and water until mushy. While hot, add marshmallows, Jello and sugar. Stir well until cool. Add whipped topping. Chill in bowl or pan until ready.

Donna Jedlicka

PUMPKIN DESSERT ROLL

3 eggs   ½ tsp. salt
1 c. sugar   1 tsp. baking powder
⅔ c. pumpkin   2 tsp. cinnamon
1 tsp. lemon juice   1 tsp. ginger
¾ c. flour   ½ tsp. nutmeg

Beat eggs 5 minutes at high speed. Gradually add sugar and pumpkin. Fold in flour. Add lemon juice and spices. Bake in greased and floured jelly roll pan at 475° about 15 minutes. Turn out on towel and roll up. Let cool.

Filling:

1 c. powdered sugar   4 Tbsp. butter
6 oz. cream cheese   ½ tsp. vanilla

Mix filling ingredients together. Unroll jelly roll and spread with filling. Roll up and sprinkle with powdered sugar. Slice and serve.

Marsha Eisenbraun

IVA'S RHUBARB KUCHEN

Crust:

1 c. flour   ½ tsp. salt
5 Tbsp. lard or short-   1 tsp. sugar
ening   ½ c. cream

Blend together flour, lard, salt and sugar. Add cream and blend. Roll out and line bottom of 10-inch pie pan.

¼ c. sugar   ¼ c. sugar
2 Tbsp. flour   ½ tsp. cinnamon
1½ c. finely cut rhubarb

Sprinkle ¼ c. sugar into bottom of lined pan. Sprinkle with flour. Put rhubarb in pan. Sprinkle ¼ c. sugar over rhubarb; sprinkle with cinnamon.

1 egg, beaten   Pinch of salt
¾ c. cream   ½ tsp. vanilla
½ c. sugar   ¼ c. flour

Beat well and pour into pie pan. Bake at 350° for 45-60 minutes or until done.

Marsha Eisenbraun

FROZEN CRANBERRY DESSERT

½ c. lemon juice
½ tsp. vanilla
1 15-oz. can Eagle Brand milk
1 8-oz. pkg. cream cheese
1 16-oz. can whole cranberry sauce

Blend first 4 ingredients until smooth. Fold in cranberry sauce. Spread mixture over vanilla wafer crust. Freeze and serve.

Vanilla Wafer Crust:
36 crushed vanilla wafers   6 Tbsp. butter
Blend together. Spread in bottom of a 9x13-inch pan.

Marsha Eisenbraun

HOT FRUIT

1 can peach halves
1 can pineapple rings
1 can pear halves
1 can apricot halves
¾ c. brown sugar
¼ c. butter
1 tsp. curry powder (optional)

Drain fruit. Mix sugar with curry powder. Layer fruit in baking dish. Sprinkle each layer with brown sugar and dot with butter. Bake 1 hour at 300°. (May add 1 6-oz. can dark sweet cherries to other fruit.)

Pamela Palmer

NEW ENGLAND BREAD PUDDING

3-4 c. cubed bread
2 c. milk
¼ c. butter or margarine
½ c. sugar
3 eggs, slightly beaten
1 tsp. cinnamon or nutmeg
½ c. seedless raisins (optional)

Scald milk with butter or margarine. Stir all ingredients together in greased 2-quart baking dish. Bake 40-45 minutes at 350°. Serves 6-8.

Variation: For chocolate bread pudding, use ½ c. chocolate bits instead of raisins and nutmeg.

Charles Harner

SPEEDY EASY CHEESECAKE

⅓ c. evaporated milk	2 eggs
1 8-oz. pkg. cream cheese	1 unbaked 8-inch graham
½ c. sugar	cracker crust
1 Tbsp. lemon juice	1 c. sour cream
½ tsp. vanilla	2 Tbsp. sugar
Dash of salt	½ tsp. vanilla

Beat cream cheese until fluffy. Add milk. Gradually blend in ½ c. sugar, lemon juice, ½ tsp. vanilla and salt. Add eggs, one at a time, beating well after each. Pour filling into crust. Bake at 325° for 25-30 minutes until set. Combine remaining ingredients and spoon over top of pie. Bake 10 minutes longer. Cool. Chill several hours.

Dixie Hustead

CHEESECAKE

1½ c. flour	1 stick oleo
⅓ c. sugar	

Blend in bottom of cake pan. Bake at 350° until golden brown.

2 8-oz. pkgs. cream cheese	1 can cherry pie mix (or any flavor)
1½ c. powdered sugar	Whipped cream
1/8 to ¼ c. milk	Chopped nuts

Blend cream cheese, powdered sugar and milk. Smooth over baked crumb mixture. Add pie mix. Top with whipped cream and chopped nuts.

Paula Blasius

LEMONADE PIE DESSERT

1 13-oz. can evaporated milk, whipped	1 small can frozen lemonade, thawed
10 oz. Cool Whip	

Mix milk and lemonade. Add Cool Whip. Pour into 9-inch pie pan lined with graham cracker crust. Refrigerate or freeze.

Carol Hammer

SPANISH WHIPPED CREAM DESSERT

½ c. butter	3 tsp. baking powder
1 c. sugar	1 Tbsp. cocoa
2 eggs	1 tsp. cinnamon
1¾ c. flour	¾ c. milk

Cream butter, add sugar and egg yolks. Beat well. Sift together flour, baking powder, cocoa and cinnamon. Add alternately with milk to creamed mixture. Beat egg whites and fold into mixture. Bake in square cake pans for 35-40 minutes at 350⁰. Split cakes and put together layers with filling.

Filling:

1 c. whipping cream	⅓ c. powdered sugar
4 Tbsp. cocoa	1 tsp. vanilla

Lucy Dill Hustead

CUSTARD PIE

4 eggs, slightly beaten	½ tsp. vanilla
¼ tsp. salt	½ recipe plain pastry
½ c. sugar	Nutmeg
3 c. milk, scalded	

Combine eggs, salt and sugar; add milk and vanilla slowly. Line pie pan with pastry. Pour in filling. Sprinkle with nutmeg. Bake at 450⁰ for 10 minutes and then at 325⁰ for 30-40 minutes longer or until knife inserted in center comes out clean. Makes one 9-inch pie.

Helen Hanewinckel

BANANA SPLIT PIE

Graham cracker crust	1 carton Cool Whip
2-3 sliced bananas	Chocolate sauce
1 qt. strawberry ice cream	

Prepare graham cracker crust according to package directions (on any box). Cover crust with bananas. Cover bananas with ice cream and then Cool Whip. Put in freezer. When ready to serve, drizzle chocolate sauce over each piece. Very good, fast, impressive dessert!

Mary Rensch

RHUBARB CHERRY PIE
State Fair Winner
Crust:

2 c. sifted flour
1 tsp. salt
⅔ c. lard
4 Tbsp. ice water

Blend flour and salt; cut in ⅓ c. lard. Add remaining ⅓ c. lard. Cut into the flour until the size of large peas. Add ice water a tablespoon at a time and mix until moist.

Filling:

4 c. cut rhubarb
1 c. sugar
¼ c. cut up maraschino cherries
2 Tbsp. cherry juice
¼ c. dairy sour cream
1 egg
¼ c. flour

Mix all ingredients together and pour into lined 9-inch pie pan. Put top crust on and seal. Bake at 425° for 15 minutes and at 350° for 25-30 minutes.

Mary Jane Hover

PECAN PIE

3 eggs
½ c. dark Karo syrup
½ c. melted butter
½ c. pecan halves
½ c. sugar
½ c. white Karo syrup
½ tsp. vanilla
½ c. broken pecans

Mix all together and pour into unbaked pie shell. Bake 40-50 minutes at 375° until set and crust is browned.

Gayle Rush

KENTUCKY DERBY PIE

½ c. margarine, melted
½ c. flour
1 tsp. vanilla
¾ c. chocolate chips
1 c. sugar
2 eggs, slightly beaten
¾ c. English walnuts

Mix in order given. Pour into unbaked 9-inch pie shell. Bake at 350° for 30 minutes.

Margaret Kuntz

CRANBERRY PIE
So easy and delicious!

2 c. whole cranberries
½ c. sugar
½ c. chopped walnuts or pecans
2 eggs

1 c. sugar
1 c. flour
½ c. margarine, melted
¼ c. shortening, melted

Spread cranberries in a well greased 10-inch pie plate. Sprinkle with sugar and nuts. In a separate bowl, beat eggs. Gradually beat in sugar. Add flour, butter and shortening, beating well. Pour mixture over cranberries and bake at 325° for 1 hour. Good served warm or cold, plain or with vanilla ice cream.

Carla Sahr

ORANGE-YOGURT PIE

1 13½-oz. can (1½ c.) flaked coconut
1 Tbsp. butter or margarine, melted

1 20-oz. can crushed pineapple (juice pack)
1 env. unflavored gelatin
2 8-oz. cartons orange yogurt

Place 1¼ c. coconut in a bowl. Toss with melted butter or margarine. Press into bottom and up sides of a 9-inch pie plate. Bake at 325° about 15 minutes or until golden. Cool on wire rack. Place remaining coconut in a pan and toast in a 325° oven about 1 minute. Set aside. Drain pineapple, reserving juice. Set fruit aside. If necessary add water to reserved to make ¾ cup liquid. In saucepan, soften gelatin in pineapple liquid. Cook and stir over low heat until gelatin is dissolved. Chill until partially set. In mixer bowl, beat gelatin mixture with electric mixer until fluffy. Fold in yogurt and drained pineapple. Pile into cooled crust. Top with reserved coconut. Chill until firm. Makes 8 servings.

Ester Johannesen

TURTLE PIE

1 pkg. German chocolate
  cake mix
1 14-oz. bag caramels
½ c. evaporated milk

¾ c. butter
1 12-oz. bag chocolate chips
1 pkg. pecans

Mix cake according to directions. Pour ½ of batter into 9x13-inch pan. Bake at 325° for 10 minutes. Melt together caramels, milk and butter. Pour over bottom layer of cake. Add layer of chocolate chips and a layer of pecans. Pour remaining batter on top. Bake at 350° for 20 minutes. Top with ice cream or whipped cream.

Ann Rush

PINEAPPLE FLUFF PIE

2½ Tbsp. cornstarch
½ c. water
1 c. pineapple juice
¾ c. sugar
1 c. drained crushed pineapple

3 egg whites
¼ tsp. salt
1 baked pastry shell
½ recipe whipped cream
  topping

Blend cornstarch and water. Add pineapple juice and ½ c. sugar. Cook slowly until thickened, stirring constantly. Add pineapple and cook a few minutes longer. Combine egg whites and salt and beat until foamy. Gradually add remaining sugar, beating until stiff. Fold into pineapple mixture and pour into pastry shell. Cool. Spread with whipped cream topping. Makes one 9-inch pie.

Helen Eisenbraun

Household Hint: For flaky pie crust, use lard rather than shortening or butter. Ice water helps keep the fat layers cold. Handle as little as possible.

80

EMPRESS PIE WITH PEANUT GRAHAM CRUST

Crust:

1¼ c. graham cracker crumbs
¼ c. margarine, melted
2 Tbsp. sugar
¼ c. chopped Spanish peanuts

Heat oven to 350°. Mix all ingredients. Press evenly into a 9-inch pie pan. Bake 10 minutes and cool.

Empress Pie:

¼ c. margarine
¼ c. powdered sugar
2 eggs, separated
½ tsp. vanilla
¼ tsp. cream of tartar
½ c. powdered sugar

1 pkg. dessert topping
1 large banana
1 oz. unsweetened chocolate, melted and cooled
1 jar maraschino cherries

Mix margarine and ¼ c. powdered sugar. Beat in egg yolks, vanilla and chocolate until creamy and fluffy. Beat egg whites and cream of tartar until foamy. Beat in ½ c. powdered sugar, one tablespoonful at a time. Beat until stiff and glossy. Fold chocolate mixture into egg white meringue. Prepare dessert topping as directed on package. Reserve ½ cup for garnish. Fold chocolate mixture into remaining topping. Slice banana into crust in a single layer. Spread chocolate mixture evenly over banana. Refrigerate 4 hours. Garnish with reserved topping and diced maraschino cherries.

Venetia Byerly

VERY GOOD PIE CRUST

3 c. flour
1 c. vegetable shortening or lard
1 tsp. salt

1 egg
1 tsp. vinegar
5 Tbsp. water

Combine flour and salt. Cut in shortening. Add egg and vinegar. Sprinkle with water. Mix together just so it holds together. Roll out. Makes 3-4 pie crusts.

Marilyn Drewitz

SOUR CREAM PIE

3 c. sour cream (if not sour, can be made sour with vinegar)
1½ c. packed brown sugar
4 egg yolks

¼ tsp. salt
½ tsp. cloves
1 tsp. cinnamon
4 Tbsp. cornstarch mixed with ½ c. white sugar
2 Tbsp. oleo or butter

Cook the above ingredients in double boiler until thick. Cool and put in a baked 9-inch pie shell.

4 egg whites
½ c. sugar

1 Tbsp. vanilla

Beat egg whites until stiff. Add sugar and vanilla. Put on top of the pie filling and brown in the oven.

Elva Hindman

TOPPING FOR APPLE PIE

¾ c. shredded cheddar cheese
¼ c. packed brown sugar

½ c. flour
⅓ c. butter

Combine ingredients and cut in butter. Sprinkle over apple pie. Bake until pie is done and topping is bubbly.

Bernice Anderson

MARSHMALLOW MERINGUE FOR CREAM PIES

3 egg whites
Dash of salt

1 c. (½ jar) marshmallow creme

Beat egg whites and salt until soft peaks form. Add marshmallow creme gradually, beating until stiff peaks form. Spread over pie to edge. Bake at 350° for 12-15 minutes.

Venetia Byerly

Household Hint: To keep cooked pudding and pie fillings creamy and prevent "skin" from forming on top, press plastic wrap directly on top of hot filling. Cool, then refrigerate, removing wrap when ready to use.

APPLE SURPRISE

1 egg, beaten
⅔ c. sugar
½ c. flour
1 tsp. baking powder

Pinch of salt
½ tsp. vanilla
1 c. diced apples
½ c. chopped walnuts

Mix well. Bake 30 minutes in greased pie pan at 350⁰. Serve hot or cold with a dollop of whipped cream and a sprinkling of chopped nuts. (Cut same as pie.)

Venetia Byerly

TOPPING FOR CAKE

1 pkg. instant vanilla
   pudding mix
2 c. milk
1 8-oz. pkg. Philadelphia
   cream cheese

1 pkg. white, yellow or
   lemon cake mix, baked
1 can crushed pineapple,
   drained
Chopped nuts
Cool Whip

Mix pudding, milk and cream cheese all together well. Pour over cooled, baked cake. Let set and then put on pineapple and chopped nuts. Cover with Cool Whip and refrigerate.

Mrs. Bill Rush

3 IN 1 ICE CREAM

1 qt. whole milk
1 c. thick cream
2 c. sugar
Juice of 1 lemon and
   rind, ground up

Juice of 1 orange
1 small can crushed pine-
   apple
2 eggs, beaten separately

Put in freezer and freeze until slushy. Add crushed pineapple and continue freezing as usual.

Margaret Quinn Rush

PISTACHIO INSIDE OUTSIDE CAKE

1 pkg. lemon cake mix
1 pkg. pistachio instant
   pudding mix (dry)
3 eggs
1 c. club soda
1 c. oil
½ c. nuts

Blend all ingredients and beat 2 minutes. Bake at 350° for 50 minutes in bundt pan. Cool. Split in half crosswise and frost center and outside of cake.

Frosting:

1½ c. cold milk
1 envelope Dream Whip
1 pkg. pistachio pudding

Blend together and whip until thick.

Betty Bauman

LEMON SAUCE

1¼ c. sugar
2⅔ Tbsp. cornstarch
¼ tsp. salt
1½ c. boiling water
1½ Tbsp. butter or mar-
   garine
3½ Tbsp. lemon juice

Combine dry ingredients. Gradually add water, stirring constantly. Cook until slightly thickened and clear, stirring constantly. Remove from heat. Add butter and lemon juice. Cool. Serve on unfrosted cakes, etc.

Marcia Sawvell

MAIN DISHES

DILLY BEEF

¾ c. dairy sour cream
1 tsp. prepared mustard
1 tsp. prepared horse-
radish
2 Tbsp. dry onion soup
mix
18 oz. thinly sliced roast
beef

12 slices rye bread
Salt if desired
⅔ c. fresh bean sprouts,
drained
12 tomato slices (¼ inch
thick)
6 dill pickle slices, cut
lengthwise (¼ inch thick)

Combine sour cream, mustard, horseradish and onion soup mix; mix well. Let stand 30 minutes. Place 3 oz. roast beef on 6 slices of bread. Season lightly with salt. Spread 1½ Tbsp. sour cream mixture on top of roast beef. Divide bean sprouts into 6 parts and place on beef. Add 2 tomato slices and 1 dill pickle slice to each sandwich. Close sandwiches with remaining bread slices.

Dorothy Hustead

BEEF BURGUNDY
(Bourguignonne)

2½ lbs. round or sirloin
steak, cubed
6 slices bacon, fried and
broken
1 can beef broth
2 c. water
½ c. red wine
2 cloves garlic, minced

½ lb. small whole white
onions, quartered
6 medium carrots, cut in
thirds
½ lb. mushrooms, sliced (or
1 large can)
2 Tbsp. flour
Wide noodles or rice

Fry bacon in large skillet. Brown cubed steak in bacon drippings. Sprinkle with salt and pepper. Add bacon, soup, water, wine and garlic; cover and simmer 1 hour. You may need to add additional water while cooking. Add onions, carrots and mushrooms. Simmer 1 hour or until tender. Stir in flour to thicken gravy and heat through. Serve over wide noodles or rice. Serves 4.

Nina Passons

SNAPPY STEW

2 lbs. beef stew, cut into ¾-inch pieces
2 Tbsp. shortening
2 c. coarsely chopped onion
1 clove garlic
1 8-oz. can tomato sauce
2 Tbsp. brown sugar
1 Tbsp. paprika
1 tsp. caraway seed
1 tsp. dill seed
1 tsp. Worcestershire sauce
¼ tsp. pepper
1½ tsp. salt
1 c. sour cream

Brown meat well in heated shortening. Add chopped onion, seasonings and tomato sauce. Cook slowly for 2½-3 hours until tender. Add sour cream. Heat and serve over platter of seasoned noodles. Garnish platter with small cherry tomatoes.

Seasoned Noodles:
3 c. cooked noodles
1½ tsp. poppy seeds
2 Tbsp. butter
Dash Worcestershire sauce

Toss noodles with poppy seeds, butter and Worcestershire sauce.

Optional: Mushrooms and small onions may replace some of the chopped onion to be added at serving time.

Evelyn Rush

BEEF STEW

1 pkg. raw stew meat
4 medium potatoes
4 raw carrots, cut into chunks
1 small onion, chopped
1 c. raw celery, cut into chunks
1 can whole kernel corn
1 small head cabbage, chopped
1 Tbsp. beef bouillon
4 c. (or more) water
¼ c. tapioca

Put meat and vegetables in a roaster. Cover with beef bouillon and tapioca. Add water, making sure the liquid covers all of the ingredients. Bake at 350° for 3-4 hours.

Lily Schroeder

CROCKPOT BARBECUED BEEF

3 lbs. brisket, browned
and fat trimmed off
½ c. chopped onion
1 small bay leaf

½ c. water
1 tsp. salt
Dash of garlic powder
1 whole cloves

Cook above ingredients 8 hours on low in crockpot. Shred beef after pouring off juices. Reserve juice. Put beef back in pot with:

½ 16-oz. bottle chili
sauce
1 Tbsp. vinegar
¼ c. brown sugar
¼ tsp. chili powder

½ Tbsp. Worcestershire
sauce
¼ tsp. dry mustard
¼ c. butter or oleo
1 tsp. lemon juice

Cook on low 2 hours. Serve on hamburger buns. Makes about 8 sandwiches. Adults will eat 2 each. Very good served with a crisp, green salad.

Susan Tillery

PEPPER STEAK WITH RICE

3 c. hot cooked rice
1½ lbs. lean round steak,
cut into ½-inch strips
1 Tbsp. paprika
2 Tbsp. oleo
1½ c. beef broth
2 cloves garlic, crushed

1 c. green onions with tops
2 green peppers, cut into
strips
2 Tbsp. cornstarch
¼ c. water
¼ c. soy sauce
2 large fresh tomatoes,
cut into pieces

While rice is cooking, pound steak to ¼ inch thick. Cut into ½-inch strips. Sprinkle with paprika and allow to stand while preparing other ingredients. Using a large skillet, brown meat in oleo. Add garlic and broth; cover and simmer 30 minutes. Stir in onions and green peppers. Cover and cook 5 minutes. Blend cornstarch, water and soy sauce. Stir into meat mixture. Cook, stirring, until clear and thickened, about 2 minutes. Add tomatoes and stir gently. Serve over rice.

Sylvia Schuler Eisenbraun

PEPPER STEAK MARINADE

2 Tbsp. oil 2 Tbsp. chopped onion (dry)
2 Tbsp. lemon juice 1 tsp. garlic salt
2 Tbsp. soy sauce 1 tsp. pepper

Mix ingredients together. Poke meat with fork. Put in mixture. Cover with foil. Put in refrigerator. Turn in mixture equal time. If in a hurry, marinade for only 2 hours. Broil.

Kathy Stone

CORNED BEEF CASSEROLE

1 can corned beef ½ lb. American cheese,
1 can cream of mush- cubed
room soup ½ c. chopped onions
1 soup can of milk 1 8-oz. pkg. noodles

Mix soup, milk, onions and cheese in saucepan on stove. After cheese melts, pour over the cooked noodles which have been mixed with the corned beef. Top with crumbs. Bake 1 hour at 300⁰. Do not cover.

Mrs. C.K. Smith

POT ROAST

4 slices bacon 1 can mushroom soup
1 tsp. lemon-pepper ½ c. chopped dill pickle
marinade 2 tsp. Worcestershire
3-4 lb. beef pot roast sauce

In Dutch oven, cook bacon until crisp. Drain off all but about 2 Tbsp. bacon drippings. Crumble bacon and set aside. Sprinkle both sides of the beef with lemon-pepper marinade. Brown meat in reserved bacon drippings. Combine mushroom soup, dill pickle and Worcestershire sauce. Pour over browned meat. Cover and simmer about 2½ hours. Remove roast to platter. Sprinkle meat with crumbled bacon. Skim fat from gravy and serve.

Gayle Eisenbraun

BEEF STROGANOFF

4 lbs. beef sirloin or round steak
Garlic powder or garlic buds
Salt, pepper and flour
Meat tenderizer
1 cube oleo
1 medium onion, chopped
½ c. water
1 can cream of chicken soup
1 c. cultured sour cream
Noodles (frozen or home-made), cooked, drained and tossed with 5 Tbsp. butter or margarine

Sprinkle steak with garlic powder or rub with garlic buds. Salt, pepper and flour both sides of steak. Pound with meat tenderizer. Cut meat into ½x1-inch pieces. Melt oleo; add chopped onion and cut up meat. Fry until brown. Add water; cover and simmer 15 minutes. Add soup and cook uncovered over low heat until thick, ½ hour. Stir occasionally. Just before serving, add sour cream. Serve over noodles.

Veva E. Wernke

STEAK RANCHERO CASSEROLE

2 lbs. round steak, thinly sliced into 2-inch strips
1 Tbsp. oil
Salt and pepper
1 onion, sliced
1 green pepper or California green chili, sliced
2 tomatoes, chopped
½ tsp. dried thyme
1 8-oz. can tomato sauce
1 c. beer
1 tsp. Worcestershire sauce
½ c. sliced mushrooms

In large skillet, brown steak in oil, turning frequently, about 15 minutes. Add salt and pepper to taste. Add onion, pepper, tomatoes and thyme. Cook 15 minutes over medium heat. Add tomato sauce, beer, Worcestershire sauce and mushrooms. Serves 6. Serve with rice or noodles, hot flour tortillas and green salad.

Pamela Brekhus McKenney

MEDALLIONS OF BEEF FORESTIERE

6 slices beef tenderloin
(each about ¼ lb.)
Salt to taste
Freshly ground pepper
taste
2 Tbsp. butter (prefer-
ably clarified)
2 Tbsp. finely chopped
shallots
1 tsp. finely minced
garlic

6 oz. fresh mushrooms
(mixture of wild and
cultivated if possible)
½ c. dry red wine
1 c. fresh or canned beef
broth (or veal broth)
¼ c. Madeira wine (or
Amontiyado sherry)
4 Tbsp. butter (room tem-
perature)

Sprinkle beef with salt and pepper. Heat 1 Tbsp. clarified butter in saucepan and add shallots and garlic. Cook briefly, stirring, and add sliced mushrooms. Cook, stirring, about 3 minutes. Add ½ dry red wine and stir. Cook until reduced almost by half and add veal or beef broth. Bring to a boil and add remaining dry red wine and Madeira. Cook until reduced by half. Heat remaining 1 Tbsp. butter in heavy skillet and add beef. Cook meat on one side for 2-3 minutes until nicely browned. Turn the pieces and cook 2-3 minutes on second side. Transfer meat to warm platter. Add mushroom sauce to skillet and stir to dissolve particles. Swirl butter into sauce. Spoon an equal amount of sauce onto warmed plates. Top each with one piece of beef and garnish with watercress or basil sprigs, if desired.

Mimi Brown

TAVERNS

1 lb. hamburger
1 large onion, browned
1 tsp. prepared mustard
2 Tbsp. catsup

1 can tomato soup
1 tsp. sugar
1 tsp. salt
1 tsp. vinegar

Brown hamburger. Add remaining ingredients and simmer for 30 minutes or longer.

Marge Lyle

TASTY BEEF AND CORN BREAD

1 lb. ground beef	1 large can evaporated milk
2 Tbsp. butter	⅔ c. water
¾ c. chopped onion	1½ tsp. salt
½ tsp. chopped garlic	¼ tsp. pepper
¼ c. chopped pepper	1 8-oz. pkg. corn muffin mix
3 Tbsp. flour	1 c. cooked peas

Brown beef in butter; remove from skillet. Add onion, garlic and green pepper; cook until onion is clear. Stir in flour. Add milk and water. Cook until thickened, stirring constantly. Add meat, salt and pepper; mix well. Place in 9-inch square pan. Prepare corn muffin batter according to directions. Pour batter in a 1-inch strip around edge of pan. Fill center with peas. Bake at 400° for 25 minutes.

Dorothy Hamann

HEAVENLY HAMBURGER

1 lb. ground beef	Dash of pepper
2 Tbsp. butter	1 8-oz. pkg. noodles
½ clove garlic, minced	6 green onions
2 8-oz. cans tomato sauce	1 3-oz. pkg. cream cheese
1 tsp. salt	1 c. sour cream
1 tsp. sugar	½ c. cheddar cheese

Brown beef in butter. Add garlic, tomato sauce, salt, sugar and pepper. Cook noodles. Combine onions (include the tops) cream cheese and sour cream. Alternate beef mixture, noodles and cream cheese mixture in layers in greased casserole. Top with cheddar cheese. Bake at 350° for 20 minutes. Serves 6.

Mrs. Thomas Roe

Household Hint: Cool and remove the layer of fat from stews or soups with a slice of bread skimmed across the top.

LASAGNA

1 lb. ground beef
¼ c. olive or salad oil
1 c. chopped onion
2 garlic cloves, minced
1 large can (28 oz.) tomatoes
2 6-oz. cans tomato paste
2 tsp. salt
1 tsp. dried basil
½ tsp. dried oregano
¼ tsp. black pepper
1 bay leaf
1 c. ripe olives (optional)
1 8-oz. pkg. lasagna noodles
½ lb. mozzarella cheese
½ c. grated Parmesan cheese

Brown ground beef in hot oil; add onion and garlic. Cook until transparent. Add tomatoes, tomato paste, salt, basil, oregano, pepper and bay leaf. Cover and simmer 1 hour or until thickened. Stir in olives if desired. Meanwhile, cook lasagna noodles in boiling salted water for 25 minutes. Grate mozzarella cheese. Spread small amount of the sauce in 9x11-inch pan. Cover with layer of noodles, arrange strips lengthwise. Add a layer of mozzarella cheese, then sprinkle with a layer of Parmesan cheese. Alternate layers, ending with sauce, then cheese. Bake at 350° for 35-40 minutes. Can be prepared the day before and baked the next day.

Mr. and Mrs. Tom Rush

CHINESE HOTDISH

1½ lbs. hamburger
1 small onion, chopped
1 can bean sprouts
1 can cream of chicken soup
1 can cream of mushroom soup
1 c. uncooked rice
1 c. chopped celery

Brown hamburger with chopped onion. Combine with remaining ingredients. Use liquid from bean sprouts and enough water to make 2 soup cans of liquid. Bake 1½-2 hours at 350°. Can be frozen unbaked.

Lily Schroeder

TATER TOT HOTDISH

1 lb. ground beef
¼ c. chopped onion
1 small pkg. frozen peas
½ c. diced celery
1 can mushroom soup
1 small pkg. tater tots

Brown ground beef in skillet and drain off fat. Add onions, peas, celery and mushroom soup. Place in baking dish. Place the tater tots on top and bake at 350⁰ for 30 minutes, or until bubbly. You can use your choice of vegetables and soups for variety.

Evelyn Rush

ITALIAN SPAGHETTI SAUCE AND MEATBALLS

1½-2 lbs. hamburger
2 eggs
1 slice bread, crumbled
1 tsp. salt
½ tsp. garlic powder
¼ tsp. pepper
1 medium onion, cut in 2 halves, then chopped
3 small cans tomato paste
2 c. water

Mix all ingredients together (except ½ onion, tomato paste and water). Shape into meatballs and fry on both sides until browned. Add remaining onion, tomato paste and water to fry pan and cook 5 minutes. Continue to simmer together for 1 hour. Add water to sauce for desired thickness. Serve over cooked long spaghetti.

Veva E. Wernke

SEVEN COURSE DINNER

2 c. cooked, diced potatoes
2 c. cooked rice
2 lbs. hamburger
1 onion, sauteed
1 green pepper, sauteed
1 c. sharp cheddar cheese
1 large can tomatoes

In a casserole, layer potatoes, cheese, green pepper, hamburger, onion and rice. Pour tomatoes over all and bake 45 minutes at 300⁰.

Frances Brekhus

FLEISH KUCHLE

2 c. flour   1 egg
1 tsp. salt   ⅔-1 c. milk
   Make a soft dough. Roll small portions into circles.
1 lb. hamburger   1 tsp. salt
⅓ c. water   ¼ tsp. pepper
1 egg   ¼ c. chopped onion
   Combine. Fill dough circles with meat. Fold over
edges; seal with a plate. Drop into deep hot fat. Fry
slowly until nicely browned. Yield: about 15 meat pies.

Delores Eisenbraun

FLEISH KEICHLA

5 c. flour   ½-1 c. water
1½ tsp. salt
   Combine to make dough firm enough to roll out. Roll
dough into 8-inch circles.
1 lb. hamburger   Finely chopped onion
1 tsp. salt   to taste
Dash of pepper
   Combine. Place about 1 Tbsp. meat mixture onto each
dough circle. Fold over and seal edges with a saucer, cutting off excess dough. Deep fry until golden brown.
Makes about 25 minutes. (I fry the excess dough strips
until golden brown—they make a great snack.)

Marsha Eisenbraun

REALLY GOOD WEIGHT WATCHER'S GOULASH

1 lb. ground beef   1⅓ c. cooked macaroni
1 Tbsp. plus 2 tsp. brown   1 c. tomato juice
   sugar replacement   ⅓ c. tomato paste
2 Tbsp. onion flakes   2 Tbsp. white vinegar
1 tsp. salt   1 Tbsp. Worcestershire
2 c. French style green   sauce
   beans   1 tsp. mustard
   Broil ground beef; crumble. Add remaining ingredients in 1½-quart baking dish. Bake uncovered at 350⁰
for 30 minutes. If sauce tends to dry out, add a small
amount of water. (2 ladies' dinner servings.)

Teresa Rush

MEATLOAF

2 lbs. ground beef   ½ c. warm water
2 eggs   1 pkg. onion soup mix
1½ c. bread crumbs   Bacon strips
¾ c. catsup   1 8-oz. can tomato sauce
1 tsp. Accent

Combine all ingredients except bacon and tomato sauce; beat thoroughly. Put in loaf pan. Lay bacon strips across top. Pour tomato sauce over all. Bake at 350°.

Frances Dean

CABBAGE PATCH STEW AND DUMPLINGS

1 lb. ground beef   1 16-oz. can stewed to-
2 medium onions, thinly   matoes
    sliced   1 15½-oz. can kidney beans
1½ c. coarsely chopped   1 c. water
    cabbage   1 tsp. salt
½ c. diced celery   ¼ tsp. pepper
    1-2 tsp. chili powder

Cook and stir ground beef in Dutch oven until light brown; drain. Add onion, cabbage and celery; cook and stir until vegetables are light brown. Stir in tomatoes, kidney beans (with liquid), water and seasonings. Heat to boiling; reduce heat and simmer while preparing dough for dumplings.

Dumplings:

1½ c. flour   3 Tbsp. shortening
2 tsp. baking powder   ¾ c. milk
¾ tsp. salt

Measure flour, baking powder and salt into bowl. Cut in shortening thoroughly until mixture looks like meal. Stir in milk. Drop dough by spoonfuls into simmering stew. Cook uncovered 10 minutes. Cover and cook 10 minutes longer. Makes 4-6 servings.

Mrs. Andy (Jo) Eisenbraun

SPAGHETTI PIZZA STYLE

1 lb. thin spaghetti	½ lb. hamburger
1 c. milk	½ c. sliced pepperoni
2 eggs	2 c. shredded mozzarella
2 15-oz. jars Ragu sauce	cheese

Prepare spaghetti as directed; drain. Beat milk and eggs together; toss with spaghetti. Spread into greased 11x18-inch jelly roll pan. Top with sauce. Crumble uncooked beef over top; put on pepperoni and cheese. Sprinkle with Italian seasoning. Bake at 350° for 30 minutes.

Pat Goldhammer

POTATO PIZZA HOTDISH

1½ lbs. hamburger	¼ c. milk
½ tsp. salt	4-6 c. raw potatoes, cut up
1 can cheddar cheese soup	

Brown hamburger; add salt while frying. Drain. Mix with remaining ingredients. Pour into 9x13-inch pan.

1 can tomato soup	½ tsp. oregano
¼ c. chopped onion	¼ tsp. pepper
½ tsp. sugar	Shredded mozzarella cheese

Mix together tomato soup, onion, sugar, oregano and pepper; pour over top of mixture in pan. Cover with foil and bake at 375° for 1 hour. Top with cheese and bake another 15 minutes.

Teresa Rush

MOM'S ITALIAN SPAGHETTI SAUCE

2 Tbsp. salad oil	2 6-oz. cans tomato paste
1 lb. ground beef	½ tsp. red pepper
4-5 small onions, sliced	1 Tbsp. chili powder
1 8-oz. can tomato sauce	1 tsp. salt
2 cloves garlic, minced	1/8 tsp. pepper
1 4-oz. can mushrooms	2 c. water

In oil, saute onions and garlic until just tender. Add ground beef; brown thoroughly. Add remaining ingredients; stir thoroughly. Cover. Simmer about ½ hour or until slightly thickened. Pour over hot, cooked spaghetti.

Gretchen Rausch

MICROWAVE LASAGNA

1 lb. ground beef	½ c. water
1 14½-oz. can tomatoes, undrained	2 c. cottage cheese
	¼ c. Parmesan cheese
1 6-oz. can tomato paste	1 egg
1½ tsp. salt	1 Tbsp. parsley flakes
1½ tsp. basil leaves	8 uncooked lasagna noodles
½ tsp. oregano leaves	2 c. (8 oz.) shredded mozza-
1/8 tsp. garlic powder	rella cheese

Brown ground beef. Stir in tomatoes, tomato paste, salt, basil, oregano, garlic powder and water. Cover with lid and microwave 4-5 minutes or until boiling. Combine cottage cheese, Parmesan cheese, egg and parsley; mix well. Pour 1½ c. tomato sauce in 8x12-inch glass dish. Place 4 uncooked noodles evenly over sauce. Top with half the cottage cheese mixture, spreading evenly. Sprinkle with half the mozzarella cheese. Spoon 1 cup sauce over cheese. Place 4 or more noodles on sauce. Top with even layers of remaining cottage cheese, mozzarella cheese and tomato sauce. Cover tightly with plastic wrap. Microwave 15 minutes, rotating dish. Microwave at 50% power for 15-20 minutes or until noodles are tender. Sprinkle with Parmesan cheese. Microwave uncovered 1½-2 minutes or until cheese is melted. Let stand 10 minutes before cutting.

Mary Jane Rush Hover

CHEDDARBURGER CASSEROLE

1 lb. hamburger	1 can mushroom soup
Onion salt	1 can cheddar cheese soup
4 c. cooked, sliced pota-	(or use Velveeta cheese)
toes (leftover or fresh)	½ tsp. oregano

Brown hamburger; season with onion salt. Pour off fat. Place all ingredients in a greased baking dish and stir (may add mushrooms or ripe olives if desired). Bake at 350⁰ for ½ hour. May add a topping of crushed cheese puffs or croutons.

Carol Hammer

SOUR CREAM NOODLE BAKE

1 8-oz. pkg. noodles
1½ lbs. ground beef
1 Tbsp. butter
1 tsp. salt
1/8 tsp. pepper
¼ tsp. garlic salt
1 c. chopped onion
1 can tomato puree
1 c. creamed cottage cheese
1 c. sour cream
1 c. shredded sharp cheese

Cook noodles in salt water, rinse in cold water, drain. Brown meat in butter; add salt and tomato puree. Simmer 5 minutes. Combine cottage cheese, sour cream, onions and noodles. Alternate layers of noodle mixture and meat mixture in a 2-quart casserole beginning with noodles and ending with meat mixture. Top with shredded cheese. Bake at 350° for 25-30 minutes. Serves 10-12.

Opal Ritzman

RICE AND MEAT CASSEROLE

1 c. rice, cooked
2 tsp. instant minced
onion
1 No. 303 can peas
1 can cheddar cheese soup
1 c. milk
2 c. cubed meat (ham, turkey, chicken, pork or beef)

Mix all ingredients together and put in 10x16-inch pan or 2½-quart casserole (I use two smaller casseroles). Put on topping (below) and bake at 350° about 45 minutes. Serves 6-8.

Topping:
1 c. finely crushed soda
crackers
3 tsp. butter or margarine, melted

Mix together.

Mrs. Erhard Eisenbraun

Household Hint: Add flavor to noodles by stirring a teaspoon of instant bouillon into the cooking water. Drain, add butter and paprika or poppy seeds.

SWEET & SOUR MEATBALLS

1½ lbs. ground beef
½ c. water
1 20-oz. can pineapple
  chunks, drained (re-
  serve juice for syrup)
¼ c. brown sugar
2 Tbsp. cornstarch
¼ c. vinegar

2-3 Tbsp. soy sauce
1-2 medium green peppers,
  cut into strips
¼ c. thinly sliced onion
1 5-oz. can water chest-
  nuts, drained and sliced
  thin

Make meatballs out of the ground beef; fry and drain fat off. In a small saucepan, combine sugar and cornstarch. Add pineapple syrup, vinegar, soy sauce, ½ c. water and salt. Cook until thick. Add meatballs and pineapple chunks, green peppers and onions. Cook 3-4 minutes. Serve over rice with soy sauce.

Bernice Chapell

LOW CALORIE HOTDISH

1 medium head cabbage,
  chopped coarsely
1 can tomato soup

1 lb. ground beef
1 medium onion, chopped
  fine

Saute onion and beef in a little butter or oleo. Heat thoroughly but do not brown. Season with salt and pepper. In casserole, layer cabbage and meat, ending with soup. Bake 1 hour at 350°.

Lily Schroeder

CABBAGE CASSEROLE

1 small head cabbage
1 lb. hamburger, fried
  and drained
1 medium onion, chopped
⅓ c. raw rice

1 pt. canned tomatoes
1 c. ketchup
1 c. water
Salt and pepper

Cut cabbage into small wedges and place in a greased casserole. Cover with hamburger, onion and rice. Pour tomatoes, ketchup and water over all. Season with salt and pepper. Bake covered at 350° for 1¼ hours.

Nyla Ghering

CALIFORNIA ENCHILADAS

1 pkg. Lawry's taco mix (in envelope)
2 Tbsp. flour
2 8-oz. cans tomato sauce
1½ lbs. ground round
1 dozen corn tortillas
2½ c. grated cheddar cheese
1 can sliced ripe olives
½ c. chopped onion

Brown ground round; drain. In saucepan, combine tomato sauce, flour and taco mix. Cook until boiling; set aside. Fry tortillas in oil, one at a time, just enough to heat through. Place 1 Tbsp. meat and tomato sauce in center of tortilla. Sprinkle onion, cheese and olives on top. Roll up tortilla and place seam side down in 9x13-inch pan. Fill all tortillas and place in pan. Pour remaining tomato sauce over the tortillas. Sprinkle remaining cheese on top. Bake 25-30 minutes at 350° until cheese on top is melted.

Nina Passons

ENCHILADA STYLE BURRITOS

1½ lbs. hamburger
24 oz. green chili salsa (Ortega)
1 can refried beans
1 c. shredded Monterey Jack cheese
½ tsp. cumin powder
¼ tsp. garlic spread
½ large onion, chopped
2 tomatoes, chopped
3 c. shredded Colby cheese

Brown hamburger, drain off grease. Add 14 oz. chili salsa and simmer until liquid is boiled out. Put refried beans in double boiler with Monterey Jack cheese, cumin powder, and garlic salt; cook until cheese melts. Spread mixture on flour tortillas. Spoon on hamburger and roll. Place seam side down in greased casserole. Top with chopped onion, tomatoes and Colby cheese. Pour 7-10 oz. chili salsa over top and bake 30-45 minutes at 350°. Serve over bed of shredded lettuce and top with sour cream.

Barbara Eilers

TOSTADO CASSEROLE

1 lb. ground beef
15 oz. tomato sauce
15½ oz. refried beans
2½ c. Doritos

1 envelope taco mix
2 oz. shredded cheddar
cheese

Brown beef; add ¾ tomato sauce and taco seasoning. Line bottom of 8x12-inch dish with 2 c. Doritos; set aside the rest. Spoon meat mixture over Doritos. Combine remaining tomato sauce and refried beans; spread over beef mixture. Bake at 375° for 25 minutes. Sprinkle with remaining crushed Doritos and shredded cheese. Bake 5 more minutes.

Jayme Hustead Chapman

FRITO CASSEROLE

1½ lbs. ground beef
1 medium onion
1 tsp. cumin
2 8-oz. cans tomato
sauce

1 tsp. chili powder
¾ tsp. oregano
2 cans kidney beans
Fritos
Cheese

Cook together ground beef, onion, cumin, tomato sauce, chili powder and oregano for 10-15 minutes. Put crumbled Fritos, then beans, then cheese; repeat. Top with Fritos. Bake at 350° until cheese melts.

Toni Schmidtlein

HOT TACOS

1 lb. hamburger
1 c. onions
Salt and pepper
1 can refried beans
½ c. regular taco sauce

¼ c. hot taco sauce
Taco shells
Shredded cheese, lettuce
and tomatoes

Brown hamburger and onion; add salt and pepper. Add beans and taco sauces. Heat taco shells; fill with above. Cover with shredded cheese, lettuce and tomatoes.

Pat Goldhammer

BURRITOS

1½ lbs. hamburger
2 pork steaks or chops
Onion, chopped
Garlic salt or 1 clove
   garlic
2 large cans tomato sauce
2 cans water
1 can whole tomatoes
1 can chilies
Tortilla shells
Chili sauce
Grated cheese
Lettuce and tomato

Brown hamburger and pork with onion and garlic. In a separate pan, combine tomato sauce, water, whole tomatoes and chilies; let cook. Add meat and continue cooking for 1 hour. Place meat mixture in tortilla shell, top with chili sauce, then grated cheese. Melt in oven and top with lettuce and tomato.

Deb Deal

VEGETABLE BURRITOS

½ c. cubed zucchini
½ c. chopped fresh broc-
   coli
1 c. sliced fresh mush-
   rooms
1 c. diced tomatoes
½ c. diced scallions
½ c. grated cheddar cheese
Tortillas
1 tsp. oil

Brown zucchini, broccoli, mushrooms and scallions in butter about 10 minutes. Remove from pan and add tomatoes. Brown tortilla in pan with oil; sprinkle cheese on top of burrito until melted. Take about ½ cup of vegetable mixture and put in center of tortilla. Add as much sauce (below) as you like and roll it up. Makes about 4 burritos.

Guacamole Sauce:
1 tomato, diced
2 very ripe avocados
2 Tbsp. chili powder
½ c. diced onions
1 tsp. lemon juice

Connie Rensch

GLAZED HAM LOAF

1½ lbs. ground beef	2 eggs, beaten
½ lb. ground lean pork	1½ c. milk
3 c. Wheaties	Pepper to taste

Mix ingredients together; press into a baking pan.

Glaze:

1 c. pineapple juice	2 tsp. prepared mustard
2 tsp. brown sugar	

Beat with rotary beater until well mixed. Pour over top of loaf and bake 1½ hours at 325⁰.

Mrs. C.K. Smith

HAM LOAF

2 lbs. cooked ham, finely chopped	1 egg
½ lb. ground pork	½ medium onion, minced
1 c. parsley, minced	2 Tbsp. glaze
⅔ c. milk	1 tsp. dried thyme
	½ tsp. nutmeg

Preheat oven to 450⁰. Combine all ingredients in bowl and mix with hands. Turn mixture onto a 9x13-inch baking dish and shape into an oval loaf. Brush with glaze and bake 20 minutes. Turn heat down to 300⁰ and bake 45 minutes more, brushing with glaze frequently. Remove from oven and brush with remaining glaze. Slice and serve. (Can be made the day before and reheated before serving.)

Glaze:

1¼ c. brown sugar	2 Tbsp. sherry
¼ c. tarragon vinegar	2 tsp. dry mustard

Combine all ingredients in food processor or blender and set aside.

Kathy Hustead

Garnish fish with lemon wedges. Dip cut edge in paprika or finely chopped parsley for an extra touch.

CONFETTI BUBBLE RING

¼ c. chopped green   ⅓ c. butter
  pepper   ½ lb. bacon
¼ c. chopped onion   2 pkgs. refrigerator bis-
¼ c. Parmesan cheese   cuits

Combine pepper, onion and cheese; set aside. Fry bacon; crumble and set aside. Cut each biscuit into quarters. Combine with pepper-onion-cheese mixture; add bacon. Add melted butter; mix well. Spoon into greased 1½-quart casserole dish. Bake at 400° for 25-30 minutes.

Gayle Eisenbraun

HAM AND CABBAGE

3-4 lb. picnic ham   Potatoes
6 qts. water   Carrots
½ head cabbage, cut up   Salt and pepper to taste

Boil ham in water for 2-3 hours; add cabbage. Cook another hour, then add potatoes and carrots. Add salt and pepper to taste. Cook until done. The longer and slower this is cooked, the better it is.

Jean Hunter

HAM-BROCCOLI ROLLS

10 broccoli spears   10 thin ham slices

Wrap broccoli spears in ham slices and place in 9x13-inch pan.

3 Tbsp. melted butter   ¼ tsp. pepper
2 Tbsp. flour   2 c. milk
1 tsp. salt   2 c. grated cheese

Mix butter and flour; blend well. Stir in milk and cook over low heat until thick and smooth. Stir in cheese, salt and pepper. Pour over ham and broccoli rolls. Bake at 350° for 30 minutes.

Colleen Clements

BARBECUED SPARE RIBS

Spare ribs ½ c. water
Salt and pepper

Lay the ribs out in a flat greased baking dish. Season with salt and pepper; add water. Bake 1 hour at 325⁰.

Sauce:

1 large onion, chopped   1 c. ketchup
2 Tbsp. Mazola oil   1 Tbsp. Worcestershire
2 Tbsp. brown sugar   sauce
¼ c. lemon juice   ½ tsp. chili powder
½ c. water   Salt

Combine all ingredients; simmer 20 minutes. Pour over ribs. Roast 45 minutes; baste ribs frequently.

Linda Rush

CALICO HAM CASSEROLE

¾ c. margarine   6 c. milk
1 c. flour   2 tsp. dry mustard
1 tsp. salt   2 tsp. Worcestershire sauce
1 tsp. pepper

Make white sauce with first 5 ingredients. Add dry mustard and Worcestershire sauce.

1 medium onion, chopped   4 pkgs. frozen mixed vege-
  fine   tables
¾ lb. sharp cheddar   2 lbs. cubed, cooked or
  cheese, grated   baked ham

After preparing the above sauce; add onion and cheese. Stir until cheese melts. Cook mixed vegetables; drain well. Add to first mixture. Add ham. Pour into 9x12-inch pan.

¼ c. margarine   1½ c. bread crumbs

Toss together margarine and crumbs. Sprinkle over casserole. Bake 40 minutes at 350⁰.

Mrs. Bill Rush

SAUSAGES AND APPLES CASSEROLE

3 very tart apples (Jon-
athan are the best)
Brown sugar
1 c. long grain raw rice
2 c. cold water (brought
to a boil)
Salt
1 pkg. best quality link
sausages (not the pre-
cooked ones)
¼ c. ketchup

Core and slice apples but do not peel. Cover bottom of 2-quart casserole with apples. Cover apples with brown sugar. Meanwhile, boil the rice in salted water. Rice will be done when water is absorbed. Cover apples and brown sugar with rice. Pour more boiling water over sausages and let stand 3 minutes. Drain. (This absorbs grease.) Arrange sausages close together on rice. Frost with ketchup and refrigerate. When ready to bake, bake at 350° for 45-60 minutes. Uncover the last 15 minutes.

Barbara Johnson

PORK CHOPS WITH DRESSING

4 pork chops
Dressing (recipe below)
1 10-oz. can cream of
mushroom soup

Brown pork chops. Mound with dressing on each chop. Pour cream of mushroom soup over all (thin with a small amount of water). Bake covered for 1½ hours at 350°.

Dressing:
4 c. cubed bread
½ tsp. poultry seasoning
Hot water just to moisten
1 small onion, chopped
½ c. butter, melted

Jane Sebade

Household Hint: Try marinating chicken in buttermilk or sour cream for several hours or overnight before frying or baking. The flavor is simply delicious and the meat is so moist!

POLISH SAUSAGE & POTATO CASSEROLE

1 pkg. Au Gratin potatoes
3-4 Polish sausages

1 pkg. frozen mixed vege-tables

Prepare potatoes as directed on package. Slice sausages thin. Add vegetables and sausage to potatoes. Put in casserole and bake at 350° for 30-40 minutes. (Can put this in crockpot and cook all day.)

Colleen Clements

CRISPY CHICKEN BAKE

1 (2½-3 lb.) frying chicken, cut up
3 Tbsp. melted fat

2 tsp. salt
¼ tsp. pepper
1 c. corn flake crumbs

Remove fat and extra skin from chicken. Rub with fat, salt and pepper. Roll in corn flake crumbs until coated. Place in greased shallow pan so pieces aren't close together. Bake at 375° until tender, 45-60 minutes.

Note: Rather than rubbing chicken with fat, it may be dipped in ½ c. evaporated milk. Do not use regular milk.

Mary Jane Hover

CHICKEN CASSEROLE

2 10-oz. pkgs. frozen broccoli, cooked
3 double chicken breasts, cooked and boned
2 cans cream of chicken soup

1 tsp. lemon juice
1 c. mayonnaise
1 tsp. curry powder
½ c. shredded sharp cheese
½ c. bread crumbs
1 Tbsp. butter

Place cooked broccoli in 9x13-inch glass baking dish. Slice chicken and put over broccoli. Make mixture of soup, lemon juice, mayonnaise and curry powder; pour over chicken. Sprinkle cheese over top. Sprinkle bread crumbs with butter over top. Bake 25-30 minutes at 350°.

Betty Morris

MARINADE FOR BARBECUED CHICKEN
(Prepare the night before)

1½ c. oil
½ c. lemon juice
½ c. soy sauce
Dash of Tabasco sauce

Garlic clove, chopped or minced
Salt, pepper and lots of dried parsley flakes

Mix all ingredients. Makes enough to marinate about 2 chickens, cut as desired. Put in double plastic bags. Tie with rubber bands and set in large bowl in refrigerator. To keep chicken coated well, just turn plastic bags at intervals. Baste with marinade while barbecuing or broiling.

Sandy Brekhus

TURKEY LEG CROCKPOT ROAST

⅓ c. flour
2 tsp. salt
¼ tsp. pepper

⅓ c. oil or fat
4 turkey legs, cut into 4 or 8 pieces

Mix flour, salt and pepper; use to coat meat. Heat fat in large heavy fry pan over moderate heat. Brown turkey in hot fat, skin side first, then the other side. Place legs in crockpot; add water. Set crockpot on high for 3 hours or low for 5 hours.

Variation: Chicken, short ribs or pork roast may be used with ½ c. barbecue sauce added when placed in crockpot.

Marie Dartt

CHICKEN IMPERIAL

1-1½ lb. frying chicken, cut in pieces
¼-½ lb. melted margarine
2 c. dried bread crumbs
¾ c. Parmesan cheese

½ tsp. garlic powder
1 tsp. salt
½ tsp. pepper
¼ c. dried parsley

Lightly salt chicken; dip in margarine. Combine remaining ingredients. Dip chicken in crumb mixture. Place side by side in foil-lined cake pan or cookie sheet. Bake at 350° about 1 hour; do not turn.

Marjorie Bielmaier

BEST EVER BARBECUED CHICKEN

1 2½-lb. broiling chicken, cut up and skinned	½ tsp. garlic powder
	½ tsp. onion salt
1 tsp. salt	¼ c. buttermilk
1 tsp. paprika	½ c. tomato puree
½ tsp. pepper	1 Tbsp. mustard

Sprinkle chicken pieces on all sides with mixture of salt, paprika, pepper, garlic powder and onion salt. Cover; let stand at room temperature 30 minutes. Combime buttermilk, tomato puree and mustard. Place chicken on rack in pan; spoon about half the sauce mixture over chicken. Bake at 350° for 20 minutes. Turn chicken; cover with remaining sauce. Bake 20 minutes longer or until chicken is thoroughly cooked. Makes 4 dinner servings.

Teresa Rush

CHICKEN SUPREME

2 lbs. chicken breasts	1 pkg. herb Pepperidge Farm dressing
1 small can evaporated milk	2 c. chicken broth (reserved after stewing chicken)
1 can cream of chicken soup	

Stew chicken; cool and remove chicken from bone. Reserve at least 2 cups chicken broth. Put chicken in 8x8x2-inch Pyrex dish. Mix soup and milk together. Spread over chicken. Mix herb dressing with reserved broth; toss well and put on top of chicken. Bake 45 minutes at 350°.

Kathy Norris

Household Hint: Fresh chicken should be used within 2 days after purchasing or defrosting. Keep it loosely wrapped in the refrigerator.

POLLO DE MARIA

8 large chicken breasts
(4-5 whole breasts)
Salt and pepper
1 medium onion
¾ small can green chilies,
diced

4 cans cream of chicken
soup
½ c. milk
1 lb. Jack cheese, grated
1 dozen flour tortillas

Season chicken with salt and pepper; bake chicken wrapped in foil at 400° for 1 hour. Bone and cut up. Saute onion and chilies in small amount of butter; add soup, milk and chicken. Layer in round shallow 3-quart or oblong 9x13-inch casserole. Start with sauce, tortillas, then cheese. Makes 2 layers. Bake at 350° covered with foil for 45 minutes. Serves 8 generously.

Mary Hustead Bottum

CHICKEN-BROCCOLI SKILLET

2 8-oz. whole chicken
breasts, skinned, split
lengthwise, boned, and
cut into ½-inch strips
Salt
Pepper
¼ c. chopped onion
2 Tbsp. butter or mar-
garine

1 10-oz. pkg. frozen cut
broccoli, thawed
1 tsp. lemon juice
¾ tsp. salt
¼ tsp. dried thyme,
crushed
1/8 tsp. pepper
3 medium tomatoes, cut in
wedges

Season chicken lightly with salt and pepper. In a 10-inch skillet, cook chicken strips and chopped onion quickly in hot butter or margarine until chicken is no longer pink. Stir in thawed broccoli, lemon juice, salt, dried thyme and pepper. Cook covered for 6 minutes. Add tomato wedges. Cook covered for 3-4 minutes more or until tomatoes are heated through. Makes 5 servings. Serve immediately.

Ester Johannesen

DELICIOUS TURKEY SPAGHETTI

3-4 c. cooked, chopped
  turkey
½ c. butter
4-5 stalks celery, sliced
1 large onion, chopped

2 15-oz. cans tomato soup
Salt and pepper
4 c. cooked spaghetti
  noodles
Parmesan cheese

Saute celery and onion in butter. Mix with turkey, soup and spaghetti noodles. Place in a greased casserole dish. Sprinkle Parmesan cheese on top. Bake 1 hour at 350⁰. This recipe is great for leftover turkey. It also freezes very well before baking. Just take it out of the freezer the morning of the day it will be baked. Serves 6.

Emma Kirby

ROCK CORNISH GAME HEN WITH MUSTARD LEMON BUTTER

2 Tbsp. softened unsalted
  butter
½ tsp. Dijon style mus-
  tard
1 tsp. fresh lemon juice

1/8 tsp. salt
1½ lb. Cornish Game hen,
  halved, backbone re-
  moved, and patted dry

In small bowl, blend together butter, mustard, lemon juice, salt, and pepper to taste. Loosen the skin carefully from the breast meat on each hen with your finger. Rub the meat under the skin with ⅔ of the butter mixture. Smooth the skin over the mixture and rub remaining butter over the skin. Roast hen skin side up on foil-lined rack of a broiling pan in preheated 425⁰ oven for 30 minutes.

Mimi Brown

Household Hint: For tasty oven-fried chicken, crush 1 cup plain or barbecue flavored potato chips and dredge chicken in the crumbs.

CHICKEN CASSEROLE

1 12-oz. pkg. chow mein noodles

1 5-oz. can water chestnuts, sliced

2 c. cut up chicken or turkey, cooked

1 can cream of mushroom soup

1 5-oz. can mushrooms, cut up

1 can cream of chicken soup

2 c. diced celery

1½ c. milk

½ c. chopped onion

Put ⅔ noodles in the bottom of 9x13-inch pan. Add chicken or turkey, mushrooms, celery, onion and water chestnuts in order given. Mix soups together with milk and pour over top with remaining noodles. Bake at 325° for 1 hour. Let stand 10 minutes before serving. Cut into squares. Makes 12 servings. You can freeze for later use but to do that, omit the soups until you are ready to bake, then add it to partially thawed casserole.

Sylvia Schuler Eisenbraun

HOT CHICKEN CASSEROLE

2 c. cooked, cubed chicken or turkey

½ c. slivered almonds, toasted

2 c. French style green beans, drained

2 Tbsp. lemon juice

2 Tbsp. instant minced onion

1 c. croutons

1 c. salad dressing (like Miracle Whip)

½ tsp. salt

½ c. grated cheese

1 c. crushed potato chips

Mix first 8 ingredients together and put in baking dish. Sprinkle with grated cheese and chips. Bake 10-15 minutes at 450°.

Joan Renner

Household Hint: Try soaking fish in vinegar and water before cooking to give it a fresh-caught flavor.

CAN CAN CASSEROLE

1 can chicken, cut up   1 small can condensed milk
1 can mushroom soup   ½ c. chopped celery
1 can chicken rice soup   ¼ c. chopped onion
1 can chow mein noodles   ¼ c. chopped pimento

Combine all ingredients. Put into greased 9x13-inch cake pan. Bake at 375° for 45 minutes. Serves 8-10.

Leila Pagel

BUFFET HOTDISH

10 slices day old bread, buttered, cubed and crust removed   1 medium onion
1 green pepper, diced
½ c. mayonnaise
Meat (one only): 2 cans shrimp or 2 cans crab or 3 c. cooked chicken or 3 c. ham or 2 cans tuna   4 eggs, beaten with 3¼ c. milk
1 c. grated cheddar cheese
1 can mushroom soup, mixed with ¼ c. milk
1 c. diced celery   Paprika

Put half of the buttered bread on bottom of 9x13-inch pan. Lightly saute celery, pepper and onion in 2 Tbsp. margarine. Add mayonnaise to vegetables. Spread vegetables over bread. Spread meat over vegetables. Add remaining bread cubes to cover. Beat eggs and milk; pour over top. Refrigerate overnight. Cover and bake at 325° for 15 minutes. Add mushroom soup mixed with milk. Spread over top. Bake at 325° for 1 hour. During the last 15 minutes of baking, sprinkle cheese on top. Sprinkle with paprika before serving.

Mary Jane Hover

Household Hint: Shrimp does not keep well so prepare it shortly after purchasing or store it in the freezer.

CHINESE CASSEROLE

1 can mushroom soup	1 can tuna fish
1 can bean sprouts	1 can chow mein noodles
1 soup can chopped celery	½ soup can chopped onion
Handful cut cashew nuts	

Mix all ingredients together, reserving part of the noodles to put over the top. Bake at 350° for 45 minutes.

Toni Schmidtlein

MICROWAVE SOLE ALMANDINE

⅓ c. slivered almonds	2 Tbsp. lemon juice
6 Tbsp. butter	2 Tbsp. dry white wine
2 lbs. dry fillet of sole,	4-5 drops Tabasco sauce
rinsed	Salt, pepper, paprika

In small glass dish, toast almonds in butter by covering dish with saran wrap and microwave about 3 minutes on high. Mix the rest with butter and almonds and pour over fish. Sprinkle with paprika. Cover and microwave on high about 6 minutes. Turn every 3 minutes. Let stand 2 minutes, then serve.

Evelyn Kjerstad

CRAB AND SHRIMP CASSEROLE

1 7-oz. can crab meat,	1 c. chopped celery
flaked	¼ c. minced onions
1 7-oz. can shrimp	1 3-oz. can Chinese noodles
2 cans mushroom soup,	½ c. slivered almonds
undiluted	

Mix all ingredients except almonds. Turn into a 1-quart casserole. Top with almonds and bake at 375° for 25 minutes.

Colleen Clements

SWISS CRAB CASSEROLE

¼ c. butter   ¼ c. flour
½ c. diced celery   1 tsp. salt
½ c. diced onion   2 c. milk
¼ c. diced green pepper

Melt butter in large frying pan. Saute celery, onion and green pepper in butter. Add flour and salt; mix well. Add milk; stir well and cook until thick.

2 c. cooked rice   ⅓ c. sliced black olives
2 6-oz. cans crab meat,   2 c. shredded Swiss cheese
   drained   ⅓ c. buttered bread
1 4-oz. can sliced mush-   crumbs
   rooms, drained   ¼ c. slivered almonds

To above mixture, add rice, crab meat, mushrooms, olives and cheese. Pour into a 9x13-inch pan. Top with buttered crumbs and almonds. Bake 30 minutes at 350⁰. If mixture is not moist enough, you can add about ½ cup milk. Serves 6-8.

Karen Poppe

CRUMBLE TOP FILLETS

1 lb. frozen fish fillets   1/8 tsp. pepper
   (cod, haddock, flounder,   ⅓ c. grated Swiss cheese
   sole or ocean perch)   1 Tbsp. grated onion
¼ c. butter, melted   ½ tsp. salt
½ c. soft bread crumbs   Dash of paprika

Let frozen fillets thaw on bottom shelf of refrigerator or at room temperature until they can be pulled apart. Place in broiler pan. Brush with a little melted butter. Broil about 3 inches from heat until fish flakes easily when tested with a fork, about 10 minutes. Meanwhile, combine remaining butter with remaining ingredients. Remove fillets from heat. Turn with pancake turner. Spread with bread mixture and broil 2-3 minutes or until crumbs are brown. Garnish with lemon and parsley and serve on a hot platter.

Dorothy Pagel

SALMON LOAF

2 c. canned salmon   ½ tsp. salt
1 c. cracker crumbs   1 Tbsp. lemon juice
2 beaten eggs   Onion juice or onion salt
½ c. milk   to taste

Remove bones from fish. Combine seasonings, eggs and milk with cracker crumbs; add to fish. Mold into loaf. If not moist enough, add more milk. Bake at 350⁰ for 40-45 minutes. Garnish with parsley. Serve with tartar sauce or other sauce of your choice.

Toni Schmidtlein

BAKED FILLETS IN SOUR CREAM

1-2 lb. fish fillets   Salt and pepper
Thin lemon slices   Paprika
1 c. sour cream

Cover bottom of shallow baking dish with lemon slices. Arrange fillets over this. Season with salt and pepper. Cover and bake until it flakes easily, about 30 minutes at 350⁰. Uncover; add salt to sour cream. Spread over fillets and sprinkle with paprika. Place under broiler until bubbly and light brown.

Venetia Byerly

TUNA CRESCENTS

6½ oz. canned tuna,   ¾ c. shredded American
    drained   cheese
½ c. chopped onion   1 can cream of mushroom
1 8-oz. can Pillsbury   soup
    crescent rolls   ½ c. milk

Preheat oven to 375⁰. In small bowl, combine tuna, onion, ½ c. cheese and 5 Tbsp. soup. Separate crescents into 8 triangles. Place 2 Tbsp. tuna mixture on wide end, roll up and fold over the ends. Bake 25-30 minutes or until golden brown. Serve with sauce made of milk, remaining cheese and soup.

Evelyn Kjerstad

SAUSAGE AND EGG CASSEROLE

6 eggs
2 c. milk
2 slices bread, cubed
1 tsp. salt

1 tsp. dried mustard
1 lb. bulk sausage
1 c. grated cheddar cheese

Brown and crumble sausage, then drain. Mix beaten eggs and milk. Break up bread, then add sausage, cheese, salt and mustard. Pour milk and egg mixture over it, then pour into a greased 8x9-inch pan and refrigerate overnight. Bake at 350° for 45 minutes. Serves 8.

Note: Do not double recipe as eggs will cook quickly around edges and will not cook in middle.

Jane O'Connell

BACON AND EGG CASSEROLE

½ c. chopped onion
4 Tbsp. butter or margarine
4 Tbsp. flour
2 c. shredded cheddar cheese

3 c. milk
1 tsp. salt
18 hard cooked eggs, sliced
3 c. crushed potato chips
1 lb. bacon, cooked and crumbled

Saute onions in butter; blend in flour. Add cheese and milk. Cook until thick. Layer half the eggs in a large 9x13-inch casserole. Pour half the cheese over top; add half the chips and half the crumbled bacon. Repeat. Bake 40 minutes at 350°. Can be made the day before and refrigerated. If cold, bake at least 1 hour until bubbly. We always have this for brunch on Christmas and Easter mornings.

Mary Rensch

———

Household Hint: Garnish ham or pork roast with peach halves.

118

CHILI RELLENO

6 beaten eggs
3 c. (24 oz.) cottage
 cheese
1 4-oz. can green chilies,
 drained

¾ c. shredded cheddar
 cheese
¾ c. shredded Jack cheese
¾ c. crushed round crack-
 ers (18)

Combine eggs, cottage cheese, crackers, chopped chilies and ½ of each kind of cheese. Turn into greased 9x12-inch pan. Bake at 350⁰ for 45 minutes or until set. Sprinkle with remaining cheese. Bake 2-3 minutes or until melted. Let stand 5 minutes before serving.

Erin Eilers

TEX-MEX EGG CASSEROLE

8 oz. Jimmy Dean pork
 sausage
⅔ c. chopped onion
⅓ c. chopped green
 pepper
8 slices day old white
 bread, cut into 1-inch
 cubes

1½ c. shredded Ameri-
 can cheese
1½ c. shredded Monterey
 Jack cheese
2 c. milk
4 eggs
¾ c. mild salsa
1 4-oz. can green chilies,
 chopped

Cook sausage, onion and green pepper until brown. Drain fat. Put half the bread cubes in a 2-quart or 9x13-inch pan. Sprinkle with half the sausage mixture and half of the cheese. Repeat layers. Combine milk, eggs, salsa and chilies. Pour over sausage mixture in baking dish. Cover tightly and refrigerate several hours or overnight. Remove from refrigerator 1 hour before baking. Preheat oven to 325⁰. Bake uncovered 50-55 minutes or until knife inserted comes out clean. Let stand 10 minutes and serve.

Carla Sahr

JIMMY DEAN SAUSAGE BRUNCH

2 lbs. Jimmy Dean pork sausage
½ c. onion
2½ c. herb or Pepperidge Farm croutons
2½ c. shredded sharp cheddar cheese
8 eggs
2½ c. milk
¾ tsp. dry mustard

Brown sausage and onions, drain. Spray pan with Pam. Spread croutons on bottom of pan. Add cooked sausage; top with cheese. Beat eggs in milk and dry mustard; pour over cheese. Refrigerate overnight.

Topping:

1 can cream of mushroom soup
½ c. sour cream
½ c. milk

Before baking, mix cream of mushroom soup, sour cream and milk. Pour over casserole and bake 1½ hours at 300°.

Joy Blunck

BROCCOLI QUICHE

1 9-inch unbaked pie crust
¼ c. grated Parmesan cheese (divided in 2)
2 c. chopped fresh broccoli
1 c. shredded Swiss cheese
¼ c. sliced small green onions
⅔ c. chicken broth
½ c. heavy cream (whipping cream)
½ tsp. salt
¼ tsp. Tabasco sauce
3 eggs

Line 9-inch pie pan with pastry. Prick bottom and sides. Bake 5 minutes at 450°. Remove from oven. Sprinkle with 2 Tbsp. Parmesan cheese. Layer half the broccoli, half the Swiss cheese and onions. Repeat with remaining halves. Beat eggs; add chicken broth, cream and Tabasco sauce. Mix well. Pour over layered mixture. Sprinkle with remaining 2 Tbsp. Parmesan cheese. Bake 10 minutes at 450°. Reduce heat to 325° and bake 20-25 minutes longer or until inserted knife comes out clean. Let stand 10 minutes before cutting. Serve.

Jane Sebade

BRUNCH EGG SCRAMBLE

¼ c. butter
½ c. chopped green
  pepper
1 small onion, chopped

2 c. sliced fresh mush-
  rooms (or 8 oz. drained
  canned mushrooms)
12 eggs, beaten

Melt butter in 12-inch skillet. Saute green pepper and onion lightly. Add mushrooms, continue to saute until vegetables are glossy. Reduce heat to medium-low. Add eggs and scramble until eggs are set. Remove from heat; set aside.

Cheese Sauce:

2 Tbsp. butter
2 Tbsp. flour
½ tsp. salt
1/8 tsp. pepper
2 c. milk

1 c. shredded cheddar
  cheese (4 oz.)
1½ c. soft bread crumbs
2 Tbsp. melted butter

In saucepan, melt butter, stir in flour, salt and pepper. Add milk gradually, stirring to blend. Cook, stirring until sauce is thickened. Stir in cheese to melt. Fold into eggs. Spoon evenly into greased 2-quart casserole. Toss crumbs with melted butter. Sprinkle over eggs. Dust lightly with paprika. Bake at 350° about 30 minutes.

Teresa Rush

BAKED OMELETTE

¼ lb. oleo
1½ dozen eggs
1 c. sour cream
1 c. milk

2 tsp. salt
¼ c. chopped green onions
Grated cheddar cheese

Melt oleo in a 9x13-inch casserole. In a large bowl, mix eggs, sour cream, milk and salt. Stir in green onions and sprinkle grated cheese on top. Bake at 325° for 35 minutes.

Betty Bauman

EGG & HAM BRUNCH

8 eggs
4 c. milk
Salt to taste
Pinch dry mustard

1 lb. cubed Velveeta cheese
1½ c. cubed ham
8 slices fresh bread,
  cubed

Grease bottom of cake pan and alternate bread and cheese on bottom of pan. Mix eggs with remaining ingredients. Pour over bread and cheese layers. Cover with foil and bake covered for ½ hour at 325⁰. Uncover and bake ½ hour. Peek in to see that cheese doesn't burn.

Marcia Sawvell

MACARONI AND CHEESE LOAF
Slices perfectly, yet is tender and moist!

1 c. 7-minute macaroni
½ lb. American cheese,
  diced
1½ c. milk, scalded
1 c. soft bread crumbs
¼ c. melted butter

1 can pimiento, chopped
1 Tbsp. chopped parsley
1 Tbsp. chopped onion
3 beaten eggs
Salt, pepper, paprika

Cook macaroni for 7 minutes in boiling, salted water; drain. Melt cheese in top of double boiler. Gradually add milk, stirring constantly. Add bread crumbs, butter, pimiento, parsley and onion. Season. Add eggs. Fold in macaroni. Pour into greased 5x9-inch loaf pan. Bake at 325⁰ until firm, about 50 minutes. Serve with tomato sauce. Serves 6.

Ann Hustead McGregor

10 MINUTE MACARONI AND CHEESE

2 c. large elbow macaroni
½ c. milk

1 10½-oz. can cheddar
  cheese soup

Cook macaroni as directed on package. Drain. Meanwhile, blend milk with soup and heat. Mix well with macaroni. Serves 4-6.

Cathie Geigle

SOUPS AND SALADS

COLD CUCUMBER SOUP

5 cans Cross & Black-
well consomme Madri-
lene
2½ large cartons sour
cream (1 pt. size)

5 cucumbers, peeled,
seeded and grated
(squeeze out extra water)

Chill consomme in cans for 3 hours or longer. Blend in sour cream to jellied consomme with wire whip. Add shredded cucumber, squeezing out excess moisture first. Refrigerate at least 2 hours before serving. Can be used as an appetizer.

Mary Hustead Bottum

CHEESE AND MEATBALL SOUP

Meatballs:

1 lb. ground beef
¼ c. bread crumbs
1 egg

½ tsp. salt
½ tsp. Tabasco sauce

Mix meatball ingredients thoroughly. Shape into medium size meatballs and brown in cooking oil. Place browned meatballs in large saucepan.

2 c. water
1 c. whole kernel corn
1 c. chopped potato
1 c. chopped celery
½ c. carrot slices
½ c. chopped onion

2 beef bouillon cubes
½ tsp. Tabasco pepper
sauce
1 8-oz. jar Kraft Cheez
Whiz

Add all ingredients except Cheez Whiz to meatballs in saucepan. Stir gently and simmer covered on low until vegetables are tender, 1½-2 hours. Before serving, add Cheez Whiz, stirring gently until blended. Serves 4-6.

Barbara Johnson

Household Hint: Glamorize a loaf of French bread by buttering and sprinkling with sesame and parsley flakes.

CHICKEN BROCCOLI CHOWDER

2 c. canned carrot slices
2 c. water
1½ c. boiled, chopped chicken
1½ c. leftover chicken broth
1 10-oz. pkg. frozen chopped broccoli
1 tsp. salt
½ c. chopped onion
2 c. milk
½ c. ground oatmeal
1½ c. (6 oz.) cubed Swiss cheese

Combine carrot, water, chicken, broth, broccoli, onion and salt in 4-quart saucepan. Bring to a boil over medium-high heat; reduce heat. Cover. Simmer about 10 minutes. Bring to a full rolling boil. Gradually add ground oatmeal, stirring constantly. Remove from heat; stir in milk and cheese. Cover. Let stand 3-5 minutes before serving. Makes four 1½ cup servings. Freezes well.

Suzette H. Kirby

CREAM OF BROCCOLI SOUP

2 c. chopped broccoli
1 small onion, thinly sliced
1 leek or green onion, sliced thin (white part only)
1 small stalk celery
1 Tbsp. butter
1-2 tsp. salt (to taste)
½ c. water
2 c. chicken broth (divided)
Pinch of cayenne pepper
3 Tbsp. uncooked rice (regular)
½ c. half and half

Cook broccoli in small amount of water and drain (reserve water). Combine onion, leek, celery, butter and water in saucepan. Place over medium heat, simmer 2 minutes. Add salt, cayenne pepper, rice and 1 c. broth. Simmer 15 minutes. Do not boil. Place broccoli, onion mix, and remaining broth in blender and blend. Combine mixtures together with half and half. Heat and serve.

Mary Jane Hover

GALLAGHER'S BEER CHEESE SOUP

2 c. milk
2 c. beer
16 oz. cheese spread
⅓ c. cooked, crumbled bacon

½ c. flour
¼ c. butter, melted
½ tsp. salt

Combine milk, beer and cheese spread in medium saucepan. Stir in bacon bits. Combine flour and melted butter; mix well. Add butter mixture to warm milk mixture. Cook, stirring constantly, until soup is thick. Makes 6½ cups. May top with croutons when serving.

Evelyn Rush

MOTHER'S CAULIFLOWER SOUP

1 head cauliflower
½ c. water
½ stick butter
1 large onion

2 Tbsp. flour
2 14½-oz. cans chicken broth
2 c. milk
1½ c. cheese

Cook head of cauliflower in water, no salt. Saute butter and chopped onions. Add flour and stir until smooth. Add chicken broth and milk. Simmer. Drain cauliflower, chop and add to liquid in soup pot. Bring to a boil and remove from heat. Add grated cheese. Stir.

Nyla Ghering

CREAM OF CARROT SOUP

1 large Spanish onion,
  chopped
4 celery stalks, grated
6-8 carrots, grated

½ gallon milk
¼ c. flour
½ c. margarine or butter
1 tsp. garlic powder

Grate together celery and carrots. Boil 3 minutes in a small amount of water. (It should be slightly cooked, still crisp.) Set aside. Brown chopped onion in margarine. Add flour; stir until smooth and bubbly. Gradually stir in milk. Add garlic and carrot mixture. Stir until smooth, slightly thickened and hot. Simmer at least 20 minutes over low heat, stirring frequently. All ingredients may be increased or decreased according to taste. The longer it simmers, the better it is.

Peggy Harner

WHITE GAZPACHO
Soup-Appetizer

3 large cucumbers, peeled and cut in chunks
1 clove garlic
3 c. Campbell's chicken broth
2 c. sour cream
1 c. plain yogurt
3 Tbsp. vinegar
2 tsp. salt
¼ tsp. pepper

Puree cucumbers and garlic in blender with some chicken broth. Then add all of the broth. Mix sour cream and yogurt. Add slowly with remaining ingredients to cucumber mixture. Chill at least 6 hours. Serve in chilled bowls. Top with chopped tomatoes, green onions, parsley and croutons for garnish. About 8 servings.

Betty Bauman

HERM'S CLAM CHOWDER

1 lb. bacon, cut up
1 onion, minced
5 carrots, diced
5 stalks celery, diced
28 oz. clam juice
3 4-oz. cans clams
6 boiled potatoes, diced
¼ tsp. parsley
¼ tsp. pepper
2 c. Half & Half
2 c. water
1 c. flour

Saute bacon, onion, carrots and celery until crisp and tender. In stock pot, combine clam juice, clams, bacon, mixed vegetables and potatoes. Add parsley and pepper. Slowly stir in Half & Half. Cook covered over low heat until heated through. Mix water and flour together. Add to chowder. Cook covered over low heat 10-15 minutes. Makes about 4 quarts.

Nyla Ghering

CUCUMBERS IN SOUR CREAM

Cucumbers
Salt
½ c. sour cream
2 Tbsp. vinegar
8 dashes Tabasco sauce
1 onion, sliced thin

Slice and salt cucumbers; let stand about ½ hour in colander. Place in a bowl and add remaining ingredients.

Carol Paulsen

HOT POTATO SALAD

6 medium potatoes   ½ c. water
6 slices bacon   ½ c. vinegar
½ c. chopped onion   1 tsp. salt
1 Tbsp. flour   1 Tbsp. sugar

Boil potatoes in jackets. Fry bacon very crisp, drain. Crumble and add to peeled, cubed potatoes. Mix flour with bacon drippings in frying pan. Add water, salt, vinegar and sugar. Cook until thick and pour over potatoes, onions and bacon. Mix well and serve hot.

Mrs. C.K. Smith

THREE BEAN SALAD

1 can French style green   ½ c. chopped onion
    beans, drained   1 bottle Italian salad
1 can wax beans, drained   dressing
1 can red kidney beans,   1 Tbsp. sugar
    drained   2 cloves garlic

Combine beans and onion. Combine dressing, sugar and garlic. Pour over beans. Set for 3 hours.

Elsie Fellers

DELICIOUS SALAD

1 can tomato soup   ⅓ c. chopped fresh onion
1 pkg. lemon Jello   1 c. cottage cheese
⅓ c. chopped celery   1 c. mayonnaise
⅓ c. chopped green pepper

Heat soup and dissolve Jello. Remove from stove and add chopped ingredients. When cool, add cheese and mayonnaise. Pour into 1½-quart round salad mold that has been oiled with salad oil. Place in refrigerator. This recipe freezes well, you need only remove from freezer and place in refrigerator the morning you will use it.

Jane O'Connell

SAUERKRAUT SALAD

1 2-lb. bag sauerkraut
1 c. sugar
¼ c. vinegar
¼ c. salad oil

1 c. chopped celery
½ c. diced onion
½ c. diced green pepper
1 small jar pimento, diced

Drain sauerkraut. In a saucepan over low heat, slowly cook, sugar, vinegar and oil. Cool. Mix all ingredients together. Refrigerate.

Donna Jedlicka

VEGETABLE SALAD

2 c. thinly sliced carrots
2 c. thinly sliced (diagonally) celery
2 c. pared, seeded and sliced cucumbers
2 c. cauliflower

1 Bermuda onion, quartered and sliced
1 pt. cherry tomatoes, halved
¼ c. chopped parsley

Toss vegetables together. Chill.

Dressing:

½ c. vinegar
¼ c. salad oil
1½ tsp. salt
½ tsp. dry mustard

1 clove garlic, crushed
2 tsp. sugar
¼ tsp. pepper
¼ c. chopped parsley

Combine and chill. Pour over vegetables and chill. Keeps well.

Elva Hindman

PATIO CORN SALAD

2 cans whole kernel corn, drained
¾ c. diced cucumbers
¼ c. diced onion
2 small tomatoes

¼ c. sour cream
2 Tbsp. mayonnaise
1 Tbsp. vinegar
¾ tsp. celery salt
¼ tsp. dry mustard

Blend the last five ingredients and pour over vegetables. Chill several hours and toss again before serving.

Colleen Clements

CORN SALAD

2 cans white corn
2 c. chopped celery
½ c. chopped green onion
½ c. chopped bell pepper

1 c. chopped green chives
½ lb. grated cheddar cheese
1 8-oz. bottle creamy Italian dressing

Mix and let stand in refrigerator overnight.

Marti Kjerstad

LINDA'S SALAD

1 can diced carrots
1 can French cut green beans
1 can kidney beans

1 small jar pimentos
1 small box ring macaroni
½ c. chopped celery
1 small onion, chopped

Drain carrots, green beans, kidney beans and pimentos. Soak kidney beans in some vinegar for 1 hour. Rinse and drain. Cook macaroni, drain, rinse well and let set for a while in ice water. Drain well. Mix macaroni, green beans, carrots, kidney beans, pimentos, celery and onion. Pour dressing over all and mix and chill.

Dressing:
2 c. Miracle Whip salad dressing

½ c. sugar
½ c. canned milk

Nyla Ghering

FRESH BROCCOLI SALAD

2 bunches fresh broccoli
1 c. sliced green olives
8 green onions, chopped
5 hard boiled eggs, chopped

Fresh mushrooms, sliced
1 lb. bacon, fried, drained and crumbled

Wash broccoli and break flowers into small buds. Toss all the above ingredients together except bacon.

Dressing:
½ c. mayonnaise
½ c. Parmesan cheese
Pepper to taste

8 oz. Wishbone Italian dressing

You may substitute green peppers or black olives in place of the green olives.

Mary Jane Rush Hover

FROZEN SLAW

1 medium head cabbage, cut as for slaw
1 tsp. salt to make salt water
3 stalks celery, chopped
1 green pepper, chopped
1 small onion, chopped
½ c. shredded carrots

Soak cabbage in the salt water for 1 hour. Drain well and add remaining vegetables.

Dressing:

½ c. water
1 c. white vinegar
2 c. sugar
1 tsp. celery seed

Boil dressing ingredients for 1 minute and pour over the vegetables. Place in freezer bags or containers. This slaw keeps frozen for 1½-2 years in the freezer or may be kept in the refrigerator for 2 weeks.

Marilyn Drewitz

VEGETABLE SALAD

1 can mushrooms
1 c. sliced celery
1 c. fresh green beans
1 can bean sprouts
1 can white corn
1 can water chestnuts
1 jar pimento, chopped
1 large onion, chopped
3-4 carrots, grated
1 green pepper, chopped
1 head cauliflower, broken up

Drain canned vegetables. Mix together with fresh vegetables.

Dressing:

1 c. vinegar
1½ c. sugar
1 tsp. salt

Mix until dissolved. Pour over vegetables and marinate overnight.

Donna Jedlicka

Household Hint: To unmold gelatin easily, rinse the mold pan in cold water and then coat with salad oil. Your mold will drop out easily and will have an appealing luster.

CAULIFLOWER-BROCCOLI SALAD

6 c. tops of cauliflower and broccoli
1 can artichoke hearts
1 can sliced ripe olives
Wishbone Italian dressing
Mayonnaise
Dill weed
Salt

Drain artichoke hearts and ripe olives; marinate with cauliflower and broccoli in Italian dressing for 12-24 hours. Drain and add mayonnaise with dill weed and salt.

Mary Jane Hover

HOLIDAY CRANBERRY SALAD

1 lb. cranberries, ground
½ c. sugar
1 lb. miniature marshmallows
1 No. 2 can crushed pineapple (no sugar)
1 c. cream
½ c. chopped nuts

Drain pineapple. Fold sugar into ground cranberries. Whip cream. Fold pineapple into cranberries; add nuts. Add marshmallows and then fold in whipped cream. You will need a 4-quart bowl to properly fold in all ingredients. Cover and chill 8-12 hours before serving.

Avis Lassegard

CRANBERRY SALAD

1 can Eagle Brand milk
1 small can crushed pineapple, drained
1 can cranberry sauce
1 8-oz. carton Cool Whip

Mix all together, adding Cool Whip last. Freeze.

Margaret Kuntz

CRANBERRY SALAD

1 qt. cranberries, ground
2 c. sugar
1 pkg. strawberry gelatin
1 c. boiling water
1 c. nuts
1 No. 2 can crushed pineapple

Cover cranberries with sugar. Let stand overnight. Mix gelatin with boiling water; cool. Add to cranberries; add nuts and crushed pineapple.

Frances Dean

CHERRY SALAD

1 egg	1 can red sour cherries
½ c. sugar	Walnuts
½ c. cream	3-4 bananas

Cook first 3 ingredients over medium heat until it boils, stirring constantly. Let cool. Add cherries, walnuts and bananas; chill.

Marlene Brown

7-UP SALAD (JELLO)

2 pkgs. lemon Jello	1 20-oz. can pineapple
2 c. hot water	tidbits
2 c. 7-Up	1 c. small marshmallows
2 bananas	

Dissolve Jello in hot water; add 7-Up. Chill until slightly set. Add bananas, pineapple and marshmallows.

½ c. sugar	2 Tbsp. butter
1 c. pineapple juice	1 pkg. Dream Whip, pre-
2 Tbsp. flour	pared
1 slightly beaten egg	Grated cheese (optional)

Mix together first 4 ingredients; cook until thick, stirring constantly. Remove from heat and add butter. Cool and fold in Dream Whip. Frost Jello mixture. Top with grated cheese if desired. Chill overnight.

Charles and Esther Hustead

FROZEN PINK SALAD

8 oz. cream cheese	4-5 bananas*
¾ c. sugar	1 9-oz. tub frozen Cool
10 oz. frozen strawber-	Whip, thawed
ries, thawed and	1 large can crushed pine-
drained	apple, drained slightly

*Toss in Fruit Fresh or lemon juice.

Mix cheese, sugar and Cool Whip. Add fruit and freeze in a 9x9-inch or 7x11-inch pan. Serve on lettuce leaf. Remove from freezer and place in refrigerator 1 hour before serving.

Sheila Gottron

RIBBON SALAD

2 3-oz. pkgs. lime Jello	1 8-oz. pkg. cream cheese
5 c. hot water	1 (1 lb. 4 oz.) can crushed
4 c. cold water	pineapple
1 3-oz. pkg. lemon Jello	1 c. heavy cream, whipped
½ c. cut up marsh-	1 c. mayonnaise
mallows	2 3-oz. pkgs. red Jello
1 c. pineapple juice	

Put lime Jello in a large pan until almost set. Dissolve lemon Jello in 1 c. hot water in double boiler. Add marshmallows and stir to melt. Remove from heat; add pineapple juice and cream cheese. Beat until well blended and stir in pineapple. Fold in whipped cream and mayonnaise; chill until thickened. Pour over lime Jello and chill until syrupy. Pour red Jello over pineapple layer. Chill until firm. Serves 24.

Linda Rush

RASPBERRY SALAD

1 3-oz. pkg. plus ¼ c.	2 c. hot water
raspberry Jello (dry)	1 c. applesauce
1 small pkg. frozen rasp-	¾ tsp. lemon juice
berries	

Dissolve Jello in hot water. Add frozen raspberries, applesauce and lemon juice. Mix well. Set overnight.

6 oz. sour cream	Chopped nuts
1 c. small marshmallows	

Mix together sour cream and marshmallows; let stand overnight. In the morning, whip well and spread over the Jello mixture. Sprinkle with chopped nuts.

Nyla Ghering

Household Hint: Store cottage cheese carton upside down. It will keep twice as long.

TWO-TONED SALAD

1 pkg. lemon Jello
1 c. boiling water

1 c. whipped cream
1½ c. cottage cheese

Dissolve lemon jello in boiling water. Cool slightly, beat with beater until light. Add whipped cream and cheese. Pour into mold and chill until firm.

1 pkg. lime Jello
1 c. boiling water
1 c. pineapple juice

1 c. crushed pineapple
⅓ c. stuffed olive pieces
⅓ c. walnuts

Dissolve lime Jello in boiling water. Add pineapple juice, pineapple, olives and nuts. Pour on top of first mixture. Let set until firm.

Marjorie Willuweit

ORANGE SALAD

1 3-oz. pkg. orange Jello (dry)
1 small can crushed pineapple

1 can mandarin oranges, drained
1 large carton Cool Whip
1 small carton cottage cheese

Mix all together well and chill thoroughly.

Margaret Kuntz

FRUIT CREAM SQUARES

1 30-oz. can fruit cocktail
1 c. graham cracker crumbs (about 12 crackers)
2 Tbsp. sugar

¼ c. melted butter
1 pkg. whipped topping mix
2 Tbsp. lemon juice
½ c. miniature marshmallows

Drain fruit cocktail. Mix crumbs and sugar in 8-inch square pan. Add melted butter. Mix and pat in even layer on bottom of pan. Refrigerate. Make whipped topping according to package directions. Beat in lemon juice. Fold in drained fruit and marshmallows. Pile into graham cracker crust and freeze overnight or 6 hours. Remove from freezer 15 minutes before serving. Serves 6.

Ann McGregor

BLACK CHERRY GELATIN SALAD

1 can Black California cherries
2 3-oz. pkgs. lemon Jello
1 small bottle pimento olives
1 c. blanched almonds

Drain juice from cherries and add enough water to make 1 quart. Boil and add Jello. When cool and slightly thick, add cherries, olives and cut up nuts.

Lucy Dill Hustead

CATHERINE'S SALAD

1 large can pineapple chunks
2 cans mandarin oranges
1 large can pears
1 large can fruit cocktail
1 c. marshmallows
¾ c. sour cream

Drain fruit for 1 hour. Add remaining ingredients. Make 4 hours before serving.

Catherine Roe

ORANGE TAPIOCA SALAD

2 3-oz. pkgs. vanilla pudding
2 3-oz. pkgs. tapioca pudding
2 3-oz. pkgs. orange Jello
6 c. boiling water
2 cans mandarin oranges (juice and all)
2 8-oz. cartons Cool Whip

Mix first 3 ingredients and add boiling water. Cook until thick. Cool. Add mandarin oranges with juice. Fold in Cool Whip. Chill about 3 hours before serving.

Marsha Eisenbraun

PINK JELLO SALAD

1 6-oz. pkg. strawberry Jello
2 c. hot water
1 15-oz. can crushed pineapple
¼ c. sugar
1 can evaporated milk
½ c. grated cheddar cheese
½ c. chopped maraschino cherries

Dissolve Jello in water. Add sugar to pineapple; bring to a boil. Add pineapple to Jello mixture. Cool. Whip in milk and fold in cheese and cherries.

Joan Renner

HEAVENLY PINEAPPLE MOLD

1 3-oz. pkg. lemon jello
1 c. boiling water
¾ c. pineapple juice
1 Tbsp. lemon juice

1¼ c. crushed pineapple, drained
1 c. shredded sharp cheddar cheese
1 c. heavy cream, whipped

Dissolve Jello in boiling water. Add pineapple juice and lemon juice. Chill until like cream. Fold in remaining ingredients. Pour into mold and chill.

Venetia Byerly

APRICOT JELLO SALAD

1 28-oz. can apricots, pitted
¼ c. vinegar
1 c. sugar
1 tsp. whole cloves

1 4-inch stick cinnamon
1 6-oz. pkg. orange Jello
1½ c. cold water
1 c. cream

Boil together first 5 ingredients for 10 minutes. Remove spices and mash or blend fruit. Add enough hot water to pureed fruit to make 2 cups if necessary. Dissolve orange Jello in this. Add cold water; cool until thick. Whip the cream and add to remaining. Chill and serve.

Evelyn Kjerstad

CHICKEN CHUTNEY SALAD

2 c. diced, cooked chicken
1 c. pineapple pieces
1 c. diagonally sliced celery
½ c. sliced green onions
¼ c. slivered almonds

⅔ c. mayonnaise
½ tsp. grated lime rind
2 Tbsp. lime juice
2 Tbsp. chopped chutney
½ tsp. curry powder
¼ tsp. salt

Toss together first 5 ingredients. Combine remaining ingredients; stir into chicken mixture. Chill. Garnish with avocado, cantaloupe, seedless grapes or fresh fruit.

Mary McCullough

NOODLE GARDEN SALAD

8 oz. medium egg noodles   1 c. mayonnaise
  (4 cups cooked)   ½ c. sliced radishes
2 c. diced sharp cheese   ½ c. diced celery
¼ c. chopped onion   1½ c. cooked peas
½ c. drained, chopped   1 c. clear French salad
  sweet pickle   dressing
1 tsp. salt   ¼ tsp. pepper

Cook noodles in large saucepan with 1 Tbsp. salt added to 3 qts. boiling water. Drain and rinse with cold water. Drain again. Combine noodles with remaining ingredients except mayonnaise; toss lightly. Cover and chill thoroughly. Before serving, gently blend in mayonnaise. Serves 6.

Cleone Naescher

SHRIMP SALAD

1 pkg. Creamette Junior-   1-2 cans small shrimp
  etttes macaroni   ½ c. diced cheese
1 c. diced celery   ½ c. diced sweet pickles

Cook macaroni, drain, rinse well and let set for awhile in cold water with some ice cubes in it. Drain well. Rinse and drain well the shrimp. Add to macaroni. Add celery, cheese and sweet pickles.

Dressing:

1 c. Miracle Whip salad   ¼ c. sweet pickle juice
  dressing   Salt
1 Tbsp. sugar   A little canned milk

Mix dressing ingredients and pour over the salad. If this gets a little dry, add a little more canned milk just before serving.

Nyla Ghering

Household Hint: The juice left from spiced peaches, pears, or apples is excellent for basting roasts or fowl.

CRAB GELATIN SALAD

2 pkgs. green Jello
2 c. boiling water
1 c. salad dressing
1 c. Cool Whip
1 can crab meat
½ c. cottage cheese

½ c. finely chopped celery
½ c. finely chopped green
  pepper
1 c. crushed pineapple,
  well drained
½ c. diced cucumber

Dissolve Jello in boiling water. When starting to set, add the salad dressing and Cool Whip, vegetables, pineapple, cheese and crab. Best if made 1 day before serving.

Gretta Rensch

CHICKEN RICE SALAD

4 c. cooked rice
4 c. cooked, cubed
  chicken
1 large tomato
½ c. chopped green
  stuffed olives

2 tsp. grated onion
1 tsp. salt
1 c. Miracle Whip
1 tsp. curry powder
¼ c. milk

Blend salt, Miracle Whip, curry powder, and milk and add to salad.

Ann Rush

TACO SALAD

1 can kidney beans
1 head lettuce
3-4 chopped tomatoes
½ diced onion

1 c. black olives
2 sliced avocados
1 small bag tortilla chips

Mix together above ingredients; set aside.
Dressing:
1 c. mayonnaise
⅔ c. taco sauce

Mix together mayonnaise and taco sauce; add to first mixture.

Frances Brekhus

139

TACO SALAD

1 lb. hamburger
1 16-oz. can kidney beans, drained
4 ripe tomatoes, chopped
1 c. coarsely grated American or Colby cheese
1 16-oz. can small pittted ripe olives, drained and sliced
1 16-oz. jar small stuffed green olives, drained
1 5½-oz. bag taco flavored corn chips, crushed
Dash Tabasco sauce
1 head lettuce
1 large onion, chopped
1 8-oz. bottle Green Goddess Dressing
1 8-oz. bottle Creamy Onion Dressing

In skillet, brown beef with Tabasco sauce. Add beans and simmer 5-10 minutes. Set aside but keep warm. Break lettuce into large bowl. Add tomatoes, onions, cheese and olives. Just before serving, add chips and meat mixture. Blend together the salad dressings and add to salad. Mix and serve. Serves 20-30.

Crystal Eisenbraun Lawrence

HOT CHICKEN SALAD

2 c. diced, cooked chicken
1 c. diced celery
½ c. chopped onion
2 hard boiled eggs, sliced
1 small jar pimiento, sliced
Chinese noodles
½ c. (1 small can) sliced water chestnuts
½ c. mayonnaise
1 can undiluted cream of chicken soup
Soy sauce (optional)

Mix mayonnaise and soup together. Add remaining ingredients; add salt and pepper to taste. Mix together and bake covered at 350° for 20 minutes. Put Chinese noodles on top and heat 10 minutes uncovered. Serves about 5.

Note: One large chicken breast yields approximately 1¾ cup cooked chicken.

Jane O'Connell

TUNA MOLD

2 envelopes plain gelatin
½ c. cold water
1 c. boiling water
2 8-oz. pkgs. cream cheese, softened
2 Tbsp. lemon juice
1 Tbsp. curry powder
1 tsp. salt
¼ tsp. garlic powder
⅓ c. finely chopped green onion (use some tops)
1 2-oz. jar pimento, chopped
2 7-oz. cans tuna, drained and flaked

In large bowl, sprinkle gelatin over cold water. Let set 1 minute. Add hot water and stir to dissolve. With beater on low, blend in cream cheese until smooth. Stir in remaining ingredients and chill until firm. Good with assorted crackers and party bread.

Venetia Byerly

CORNED BEEF SALAD

1 pkg. lemon Jello
1 c. hot water
½ c. cold water
1 can corned beef, broken up
1 c. diced celery
1 Tbsp. chopped onion
2 Tbsp. chopped green pepper
1 pimento, chopped
2 Tbsp. horseradish
1 c. Miracle Whip

Dissolve lemon Jello in hot water; add cold water. While Jello cools, mix other ingredients. Add Jello. Pour into glass pan. Refrigerate. Serves 8-10.

Whipped Horseradish Cream:

1 c. heavy cream
1 Tbsp. bottled horse-radish
¼ tsp. Worcestershire sauce
Dash liquid red pepper
Seasonings

Combine. In a small bowl, whip until soft peaks form.

Evelyn Rush

Household Hint: A lemon will yield one to two tablespoons more juice if first heated in hot water.

BLT SALAD

1 lb. bacon, cooked and crumbled

1 head leaf lettuce, chopped

Cherry tomatoes, halved

2 lbs. broccoli flowerettes

1 medium red onion, chopped

In glass bowl, layer above ingredients in order given (use only half of each ingredient). Repeat in same order.

Dressing:

1 c. mayonnaise

½ c. Parmesan cheese

1 Tbsp. sugar

Mix together. Put on top of ingredients and cover with clear plastic wrap. Refrigerate 12 hours or overnight. Toss before serving. Serves 3-4.

Marjorie Hustead

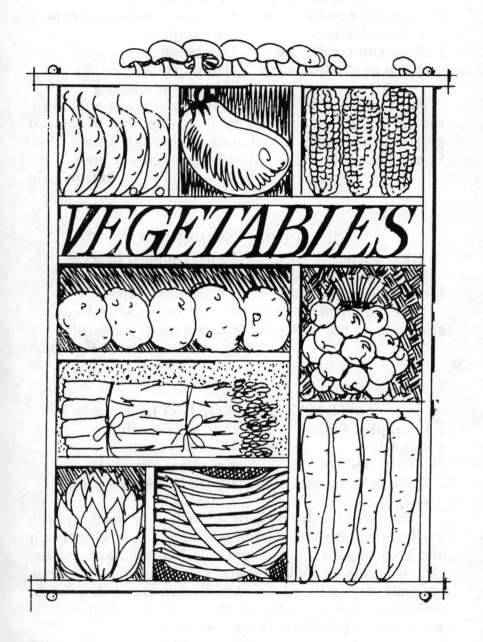

SUMMER SQUASH CASSEROLE

2 c. cooked zucchini, cut
  in ¾ inch slices
1 10-oz. can condensed
  cream of chicken soup

½ c. cultured sour cream
  or yogurt
Dry bread
Grated cheese
Paprika and butter

Place zucchini in 4 small dishes and cover with mixture of soup and sour cream. Top with dry bread and grated cheese and a little paprika. Then dot with butter. Bake about 7 minutes of until thoroughly heated.

Marge Lyle

BROCCOLI CASSEROLE

½ stick butter
⅓ c. chopped onion
1 can mushroom soup

10 oz. chopped broccoli
24 oz. Cheez Whiz
1½ c. cooked rice

Thaw chopped broccoli. Mix all ingredients together and bake 35 minutes at 350⁰ in a 2-quart casserole.

Mrs. C.K. Smith

TOMATOES FLORENTINE

1 10-oz. pkg. frozen
  spinach
1½ Tbsp. butter
2 Tbsp. dehydrated onion
  soup mix

½ c. sour cream
1 Tbsp. yogurt
4 medium tomatoes
1 hard boiled egg yolk,
  sieved

Combine spinach and butter; cook over medium heat until spinach is thawed. Add onion soup mix, sour cream and yogurt. Heat, but do not allow to boil. Meanwhile, slice off ends of tomatoes and scoop out centers; rinse and pat dry. Fill with spinach mixture and bake in preheated 350⁰ oven for 15-20 minutes until tomatoes are tender. Sprinkle with egg yolk and serve.

Mary Ann Fournier

DELICIOUS BAKED BEANS

2 lbs. navy beans
1 lb. diced ham
2 c. brown sugar
1 c. catsup
½ c. molasses

¼ tsp. ginger
1 Tbsp. prepared mustard
1 onion, diced
Salt and pepper to taste

Soak beans and ham overnight, then boil until skins pop. Combine beans and ham with brown sugar, catsup, molasses, ginger, mustard and onion. Add salt and pepper to taste. Place mixture into baking dish and bake at 300° for 4-5 hours. Bake uncovered the last hour.

Jean Hunter

DELICIOUS EGGPLANT

Eggplant
Chopped onions

Mayonnaise
Parmesan cheese

Cut eggplant crosswise about ½ inch thick. Soak slices to cover in cold salted water for 20 minutes; drain well. Spread each slice generously with mayonnaise and top with lots of chopped onions. Place on cookie sheet and bake at 300° for 20 minutes. Remove from oven and sprinkle each slice with Parmesan cheese. Broil until golden.

Sandy Brekhus

BROCCOLI CASSEROLE

3 pkgs. frozen broccoli,
  cooked as directed
1 stick margarine
1 onion, chopped
1 can cream of celery
  soup

1 can cheddar cheese soup
1 egg
½ c. mayonnaise
2 c. Pepperidge Farm stuffing mix

Mix onion, soups, egg and mayonnaise together. Pour over broccoli. Melt butter and toss in stuffing mix. Put stuffing on top of broccoli. Bake 20 minutes at 350° in cake pan.

Kathy Norris

ESCALLOPED EGGPLANT OR ZUCCHINI

1 medium eggplant or zucchini, diced

3 medium onions, diced
¼ c. butter

Boil eggplant or zucchini with onion in salt water until tender but not mushy. Drain well and add butter; let mixture cool. Then add:

1 c. milk
3 beaten eggs
¼ lb. (1 pkg.) rolled white crackers

1 tsp. baking powder
1 c. grated cheese (or use 1 can Campbell's cheddar cheese soup)

Mix with above. Place in greased casserole. Bake about 1 hour at 350⁰.

Marjorie Bielmaier

ITALIAN GREEN BEANS

6 slices bacon
1 large onion
2 cans Italian green beans, drained

1 can undiluted tomato soup
½ c. brown sugar

Fry bacon and onion together. Mix all together and bake for 2½ hours at 325⁰.

Connie Rensch

ZUCCHINI

2 medium zucchini
½ tsp. celery seed
½ tsp. garlic powder

¾ c. grated sharp cheese
½ tsp. salt

Peel zucchini and slice into 1-inch rounds. Place in 9-inch round glass pan. Sprinkle celery seed, salt, and garlic powder over all. Place in microwave for 9 minutes. Remove and sprinkle cheese on top. Return to microwave for 3 minutes more.

Bernice Chapell

GARDEN VEGETABLE CASSEROLE

1 tsp. minced garlic	¼ lb. bacon, cut into 1-inch
1½ tsp. salt	lengths
¼ tsp. pepper	2 lbs. zucchini, diced
1 tsp. basil	1 large onion, cut in wedges
1 6-oz. pkg. Swiss cheese	1 Tbsp. flour
1 c. slivered almonds	2 c. diced fresh tomatoes
	or 1 1-lb. can

Saute almonds and bacon until crisp; remove from skillet. Add zucchini and onion. Cook over medium heat for 15 minutes. Mix in flour, tomatoes and spices. Layer vegetables, then almonds and bacon and then cheese slices, ending with bacon and almonds. Serve immediately or bake uncovered at 400° for 15 minutes.

Evelyn Kjerstad

VEGETABLE PIZZA

2 pkgs. crescent rolls	1 pkg. Mrs. Grass or Knorr
Cream cheese, softened	vegetable soup mix
16 oz. sour cream	

Pat crescent rolls into jelly roll pan. Bake 10 minutes at 375° and cool. Spread a thin layer of softened cream cheese on crust. Mix together sour cream and vegetable soup mix. Spread over cream cheese. Layer the following:

1½ c. cauliflower	Sliced radishes
1½ c. broccoli	1½ c. tomatoes
1½ c. celery	¾ c. green pepper
¾ c. olives	Shredded cheese (on top)
½ c. shredded carrots	

Cut into squares and enjoy. I put all the vegetables in the food processor.

Mary Jane Rush Hover

DEEP FAT FRIED ZUCCHINI

1½ lbs. zucchini	2 eggs
Salt and pepper	¼ c. milk
¼ c. flour	Bread crumbs

Cut zucchini into about 1½-inch cubes. Beat eggs, flour and milk together. Season zucchini with salt and pepper. Roll in flour, then dip into egg mixture, then roll in bread crumbs. Fry in deep fat until golden brown.

Evelyn Kjerstad

ZUCCHINI BAKE

4-6 c. thinly sliced zucchini	1 clove garlic, finely chopped
¼-½ c. chopped onion	1 c. Bisquick
½ c. grated cheese	½ c. vegetable oil
1 Tbsp. parsley	3 eggs, slightly beaten
¾ tsp. salt	Parmesan cheese
Shake of oregano	

Mix all ingredients except Parmesan cheese. Put in greased 9x13-inch pan. Sprinkle with Parmesan cheese. Bake at 350° for 30 minutes.

Kelly Engelhart

SWISS GREEN BEANS

¼ c. oleo	1 tsp. sugar
½ c. corn flake crumbs	1 8-oz. carton sour cream
2 Tbsp. flour	4 cans French style green beans, drained
1 tsp. salt	
1 tsp. pepper	2 c. shredded Swiss cheese
¼ tsp. minced onion	

Melt 2 Tbsp. oleo, add corn flakes and set aside. Melt 2 Tbsp. oleo over low heat; stir in flour, salt, pepper, onion and sugar. Add sour cream; stir until smooth. Cook until thickened; fold in green beans. Spread mixture into greased 10x6x2-inch baking dish. Sprinkle cheese over top. Sprinkle corn flake crumbs over cheese. Bake uncovered 20 minutes at 400°.

Ann Rush

GREEN RICE

1½ c. raw Minute Rice	1 small jar Cheez Whiz
1 can cream of mush- room soup	1 stick oleo, melted ½ c. chopped celery
1 pkg. frozen broccoli, thawed	½ c. chopped onion

Bake at 350⁰ for 40 minutes.

Donna Jedlicka

SCALLOPED CORN

1 qt. drained corn	2 eggs, beaten
1 c. cracker crumbs	2 Tbsp. butter, melted
⅓ c. diced celery	¼ tsp. paprika
¼ c. diced onion	1 c. milk
½ c. diced Velveeta cheese	1 tsp. salt

Combine ingredients and place in a 2-quart casserole or baking dish. Bake at 350⁰ for 50-60 minutes. Cover for the first ½ hour of baking time, then uncover to let it brown.

Marilyn Huether

BAKED BEANS

½-1 lb. ground beef	½ lb. diced bacon

Brown ground beef and bacon; drain off fat. Add:

1 can pork and beans, undrained	¼ c. mustard ¼-½ c. catsup
1 can kidney beans, undrained	2 Tbsp. sugar ¾ c. brown sugar
1 can butter beans, un- undrained	2 Tbsp. molasses

Mix all together and bake uncovered at 350⁰ for 35-40 minutes.

Marjorie Hustead

POTATO KUKEL

6 c. grated potatoes	Salt and pepper to taste
2 c. chopped onion	¼ c. butter
⅓ c. butter	Sour cream
3 eggs	

Saute onions in ⅓ c. butter; add to potatoes. Slightly beat eggs and mix with potatoes and onion. Season with salt and pepper to taste. Melt ¼ c. butter in large iron skillet, add potato mixture. Bake at 400⁰ for 1 hour. To serve, cut into pie-shaped wedges. Top with sour cream.

Joan Renner

HOLIDAY SWEET POTATOES

3 large sweet potatoes or yams	2 eggs
2-3 Tbsp. butter	½ tsp. cinnamon
⅔ c. milk	½ tsp. nutmeg

Wash and dry potatoes, then wrap them in foil. Bake potatoes about 1 hour at 400⁰ or until tender. Cool until easy to handle. Remove skins and cut potatoes up. Using a mixer, food processor or blender, mix potatoes with butter, milk, eggs, cinnamon and nutmeg. Mix or blend until creamy and smooth. Put in a casserole dish with a lid. Bake at 375⁰ for 15 minutes or until mixture is thoroughly heated. To keep the creamy texture, cover with foil and a lid.

Marilyn Huether

LIMA BEANS IN CREAM

2½ c. lima beans	2 tsp. salt
½ c. butter	3 Tbsp. molasses
½ c. brown sugar	1 c. sour cream

Soak beans overnight. Cook in salt water just until tender; drain and rinse well in water. Work in butter while hot. Mix brown sugar and salt through beans. Add sour cream and molasses. Bake at 300⁰ for 1 hour. Serves 8-12.

Opal Ritzman

COMPANY POTATOES

½ c. butter, softened
1 can cream of mush-
room or cream or
celery soup
1 c. chopped green onion
2 c. grated cheese

1 pt. sour cream
1 2-lb. pkg. frozen South-
ern style hash browns,
thawed
Crushed potato chips

Combine butter, soup, onion and sour cream (reserve some for topping) in a 9x13-inch dish. Stir in potatoes. Top with remaining liquid mixture, grated cheese and crushed potato chips. Bake at 350° for 1 hour. Serves 6-8.

Nyla Ghering

POTATO BAKE

16 oz. sour cream
1 can cream of chicken
soup
Salt and pepper
1 stick margarine

1 2-lb. pkg. Ore-Ida chunky
hash browns
3 c. grated cheese (½ Mon-
tery and ½ cheddar)
1 onion, diced

Mix together first 4 ingredients. Mix together remaining ingredients. Pour first mixture over potato mixture. Pour into 9x13-inch pan. Bake at 350° for 1 hour.

2 c. crushed corn flakes   ½ stick oleo, melted

Mix together and put on top and bake ½ hour longer.

Mildred Rush

GREEN BEAN CASSEROLE

1 20-oz. bag French style
green beans, cooked
1 medium onion, chopped
1 c. sour cream
1 Tbsp. sherry

1 c. shredded sharp ched-
dar cheese
1 c. buttered, browned
bread crumbs

Saute onions in butter. Add sour cream and sherry. Mix with green beans. Top with cheese and bread crumbs. Bake at 325° for 30 minutes.

Suzette H. Kirby

BEST BACKYARD BEANS

3 slices bacon, cut in half	1 c. catsup
2 16-oz. cans pork and beans	1 medium onion, chopped
	¼ c. Worcestershire sauce
1 c. packed brown sugar	2 Tbsp. prepared mustard

Partially fry bacon, remove and set aside. In a 2-quart casserole, combine all other ingredients. Lay partially cooked bacon on top. Bake uncovered at 350° about 2 hours.

Venetia Byerly

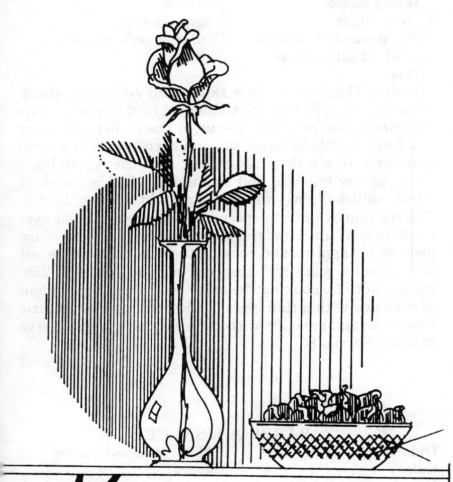

MISCELLANEOUS

APFELPFANNKUCHEN
(German Apple Pancakes)

6 Tbsp. butter
4 tart apples, peeled and thinly sliced
½-¾ c. sugar
1 tsp. ground cinnamon
1 c. sifted all-purpose flour
2 tsp. grated lemon rind
¼ tsp. salt
1 c. milk
2 eggs, beaten
Confectioner's sugar

Melt 4 Tbsp. butter in a skillet and add apple slices. Cook slowly until tender. Add lemon rind, sugar to taste and cinnamon; mix well. Leave in the skillet over very low heat. Combine flour, salt, milk and eggs in a bowl and stir with a fork until smooth. Add the remaining 2 Tbsp. butter (melted) and mix again. Heat a 7-inch or 8-inch skillet (lightly greased) and add 3 Tbsp. batter. Tilt the pan at once to spread batter evenly. Cook over medium heat until underside of pancake is golden. Turn over with a spatula and cook on the other side. Turn out onto a warm plate and keep warm in a preheated 250⁰ oven. Continue cooking the other pancakes. Spread half of each one with a thin layer of the warm apple mixture. Fold over and sprinkle with confectioner's sugar. Serve at once. Serves 8.

Dorothy Pagel

BARBEQUE SAUCE

Onions
Celery
¼ c. butter
2 Tbsp. vinegar
2 Tbsp. Worcestershire sauce
3 Tbsp. brown sugar
1 c. tomato juice or soup

Brown onions, celery, brown sugar and butter. Add vinegar, Worcestershire sauce and tomato juice. Pour over meat. Bake.

Margaret Wittmer

SWEET-HOT MUSTARD

1 c. sugar   1 can dry mustard
1 c. cider   2 eggs

Whip together sugar, cider and dry mustard. Let stand overnight. Place in double boiler. Whip eggs and add to mustard. Bring to a boil. Stir until thick.

Frances Brekhus

SWEET AND SOUR SAUCE FOR HAM

1 c. cider vinegar   1 Tbsp. flour
1 c. brown sugar   4 eggs
3 Tbsp. dry mustard   1 jar currant jelly

Place all ingredients in a double boiler. Mix and let it cook over medium heat until it is the consistency of applesauce. Takes about an hour. Can be kept in refrigerator for three weeks. So delicious as an accompaniment to ham.

Peggy Kirby

CARROT-CUKE RELISH

3½ c. coarsely ground unpeeled cucumbers   2 Tbsp. salt
1½ c. coarsely ground carrots   2 c. sugar
1½ c. vinegar
1 c. coarsely ground onions   1½ tsp. celery seed
1 tsp. mustard seed

Mix ground vegetables and salt. Let stand 3 hours and drain. In large pan, combine remaining ingredients. Bring to a boil. Add vegetables and simmer 20 minutes. Can be canned or cooled and kept in refrigerator. Makes 2½ pints.

Venetia Byerly

RHUBARB JELLY

10 c. cut up rhubarb   3 pkgs. strawberry Jello
6 c. sugar

Combine rhubarb and sugar; let stand overnight. In the morning, bring mixture to a boil and simmer 15 minutes. Add strawberry Jello. Stir until well mixed. Put into jars and seal.

Donna Jedlicka

CRANBERRY CHUTNEY

3½ c. sugar
1 c. cider vinegar
1¼ c. chopped fresh
onions
1 c. currants
1 tsp. allspice

3 Tbsp. finely grated
ginger root
5 c. fresh whole cran-
berries
1 c. chopped walnuts,
pecans or almonds

In a large saucepan, combine sugar, vinegar, onion, currants, allspice and ginger root. Cook over medium heat until sugar dissolves. Add cranberries and cook for 10 minutes or until berries have popped. Add nuts. Pour into sterilized jars and seal with paraffin or freeze. Makes about 2 quarts.

Note: Makes a wonderful appetizer when spooned over a block of cream cheese and accompanied with rye crackers.

Carla Sahr

PICKLED BEETS

Small beets
2 c. sugar
2 c. water
2 c. vinegar

3 inch stick cinnamon
1 tsp. whole cloves
½ tsp. allspice

Cook small beets until tender. Slip off skins. Slice beets if the beets are larger than desired. Make a pickling syrup of remaining ingredients. Spices may be tied in a bag. Cover beets and cook with mixture. Simmer 15 minutes. Pack in clean hot jars and seal.

Bernice Chapell

LIME PICKLES

7½ lbs. cucumbers, cut   2 c. lime
  ½ inch thick   2 gal. water

Prepare cucumbers. Mix lime and water; let cucumbers stand in it for 24 hours. Rinse well. Let stand in cold water for 3 hours; drain.

Syrup:

2 qts. vinegar   1 tsp. mixed pickling spice
10 c. sugar   1 tsp. salt
1 tsp. whole cloves

Pour syrup mixture over while cold. Let stand overnight. Then boil for 40 minutes. Pour into sterilized jars and seal.

Claramae White

DILL PICKLES

1 gal. water   Dill
1 c. vinegar   Mixed pickling spices
1 tsp. alum   Garlic
1 c. pickling salt   Sweet or sharp peppers
Dill-sized cucumbers   (optional)

Bring first 4 ingredients to a boil. Boil about 10 minutes. Let cool until cold. Pack cucumbers in jars with dill, ½ tsp. mixed pickling spice, 1-2 pieces garlic and peppers if desired. Pour syrup over cucumbers. Partially seal. Let set at room temperature for 7-10 days, then finish sealing and store where it's cool.

Helen L. Eisenbraun

CARAMELS

2 c. sugar   1 c. milk
1¾ c. dark corn syrup   ½ c. nuts
1 c. cream   1 tsp. vanilla
1 c. butter

Bring to a boil sugar, syrup, butter and cream. Add milk. Bring to hard ball stage. Add vanilla and nuts. Pour into a buttered pan.

Mrs. Charles Pagel

SUZIE'S TRUFFLES

1 lb. good semi-sweet
  chocolate
1 c. cream

3 Tbsp. Grand Marnier
¼ c. Droste's cocoa
Cinnamon

Chop chocolate into coin-sized pieces. Bring cream to a boil. Pour over chocolate. Stir until smooth. Add Grand Marnier. Chill overnight. Scoop into balls. Roll in Droste's cocoa that has been sprinkled with cinnamon. Place on cookie sheets covered with waxed paper. Refrigerate until hard. Store in refrigerator in covered container.

Jayme Hustead Chapman

KNOX BLOX GELATINE SNACKS

4 envelopes Knox unfla-
  vored gelatine

3 3-oz. pkgs. flavored
  gelatin
4 c. boiling water

In large bowl, combine Knox unflavored gelatine and flavored gelatin. Add boiling water and stir until gelatin dissolves. Pour into large shallow baking pan (9x13-inch) and chill until firm. Cut into squares to serve. Makes about 100 one-inch squares. These can be left setting on the cupboard and will not melt. Can easily be picked up with fingers and eaten.

Ester Johannesen

MICROWAVE CARAMEL CORN

1 stick oleo
¼ c. dark Karo syrup
1 c. packed brown sugar

½ tsp. soda
8-10 c. popped corn

Put oleo, syrup and brown sugar in microwave dish. Heat for 1½ minutes, stir and then cook until mixture boils. Stir in soda. Pour over popcorn and mix well. Put in large paper bag and microwave for 1½ minutes. Shake the corn and microwave for 1½ minutes more. Pour onto a cookie sheet to cool.

Hazel Whitwer

OVEN CARAMEL CORN

7-8 qts. popped corn
2 c. salted peanuts
  (optional)
1 c. brown sugar
1 c. white sugar
1 c. oleo or butter

½ tsp. salt
½ c. white corn syrup
1 tsp. vanilla
1 tsp. butter flavoring
1 tsp. soda

Place popped corn and salted nuts in a large container. In saucepan, combine sugars, butter, salt and flavoring. Bring to a boil. Boil 5 minutes, stirring occasionally. Remove from heat and add soda. Stir quickly. Pour over popcorn and mix. Place popcorn mix in large flat pans. Bake at 250° for 1 hour, stirring several times. Remove from oven and stir occasionally while mixture cools. Store in airtight container.

Elva Hindman

BUTTERMILK FUDGE

2 c. sugar
½ c. butter or oleo
1 c. buttermilk
1 tsp. soda

2 Tbsp. white syrup
1 tsp. vanilla
½ c. chopped nuts

Dissolve soda in buttermilk. Cook sugar, butter, buttermilk, soda and syrup until soft ball stage. Add vanilla and beat. Add chopped nuts. Put in greased 8x8-inch pan. Candy foams up as it boils and turns brown. Watch for scorching.

Evelyn Kjerstad

EASY CREAMY FUDGE

1 lb. Velveeta cheese
1 lb. oleo
4 lbs. powdered sugar

1 c. cocoa
1 Tbsp. vanilla
4 c. chopped nuts

Melt cheese and oleo together. Mix in remaining ingredients. Pour mixture into shallow pan and spread. Cool and cut into small pieces. Makes 7 pounds of candy.

Elva Hindman

QUICKIE FUDGE (MICROWAVE)

1 lb. sifted powdered
   sugar
½ c. cocoa
¼ c. milk
¼ lb. butter or oleo (½ c.)

1 Tbsp. vanilla
½ c. chopped nuts
½ c. miniature marsh-
   mallows

Blend powdered sugar and cocoa in mixing bowl. Add milk, butter and marshmallows, but do not mix. Cook in microwave 3 minutes on high. Remove and stir to mix ingredients. Add vanilla and nuts; mix until blended. Pour into greased containers and place in freezer for 20 minutes or refrigerate for 1 hour. Cut and serve.

Elva Hindman

AMERICAN TAFFY

½ c. butter
2 c. white sugar
1¼ c. light corn syrup

1½ c. water
1/8 tsp. cream of tartar

Melt butter; add sugar mixed with cream of tartar. Add remaining ingredients. Stir until sugar is dissolved. Cook to hard ball stage. Pour into greased platters. Butter hands and pull from one hand to other. Soon it will become white. Pull into thin strips. Lay on greased surface. When hard, break into bite-size pieces and eat.

Bernice Chapell

MICROWAVE PEANUT BRITTLE

⅔ c. raw peanuts
1 c. sugar
½ c. white corn syrup
1/8 tsp. salt

1 tsp. baking soda
1 tsp. vanilla
1 tsp. butter

In a 2½-quart casserole, stir together peanuts, sugar, syrup and salt. Cook 8 minutes on high, stirring well after 4 minutes. Add butter and vanilla. Cook 1 more minute on high. Add baking soda and quickly stir until light and foamy. Immediately pour into lightly buttered baking sheet. Spread thin. When cool, break into pieces.

Donna Jedlicka

SWEDISH NUTS

1 lb. nuts (pecans, almonds or walnuts)
1 c. sugar
½ tsp. salt
2 stiffly beaten egg whites
½ c. butter

Toast nuts in a 325° oven until light brown. Fold sugar and salt into egg whites. Beat until stiff peaks form. Fold in nuts. Melt butter in large cake pan. Spread nut mixture in this and bake at 325° about 30 minutes. Stir every 10 minutes. Cool.

Carol Paulsen

EAGLE BRAND MILK

½ c. warm water
1 c. plus 2 Tbsp. powdered sugar
¾ c. sugar
1 c. plus 2 Tbsp. powdered milk

Dissolve water and milk in top of double boiler. Add sugar and cook until thick, stirring constantly.

Elva Hindman

JERKY

Morton's Tender Quick
pepper
Wright's liquid smoke
Window screen for oven racks

Bone and carefully trim meat. Freeze to crystal stage and slice about 1/8 inch thick. Using a glass bowl or pan, lay slices to cover bottom. With a pastry brush, apply a light coat of liquid smoke. Sprinkle on Tender Quick (enough to give it a dull look—a big kitchen shaker works well). Just a sprinkle of pepper is enough. Continue to layer in opposite directions each time until the bowl is full. Cover and refrigerate about 12 hours. Place marinated meat on a window screen the size of oven rack. Place in oven and dry for 3-4 hours at lowest oven temperature. It is okay to marinate several batches at a time as it keeps well in refrigerator. When dry, store in fairly airtight container and freeze.

Marcia Sawvell

KNAPFLA (BUTTONS)

3 c. flour

1 tsp. salt

3 eggs

Milk or water enough to make fairly stiff dough

Sift flour with salt. Add eggs and milk or water to make fairly stiff dough. Boil about 6 c. water in kettle. Add salt to taste. Cut Knapfla into boiling water with scissors. Cook as for noodles, about 5-8 minutes after they've started boiling. Drain.

Helen Eisenbraun

PIZZA CRUST

2 pkgs. yeast

7-8 c. flour

1 tsp. salt

2½ c. warm water

Combine yeast, 2½ c. flour, salt and water. Beat at low speed for 30 seconds, then 3 minutes at high speed. Stir in enough flour to make moderately stiff dough. Knead 8-10 minutes until smooth. Put in bowl to rise until doubled, 45 minutes. Punch down. Divide into fourths (I usually get 5). Roll out each section and put on ungreased cookie sheet. Bake at 450° for 6-8 minutes until it starts to brown. Cool. Put topping on as your family desires. Can wrap and freeze at this stage. Bake at 350° for 20-25 minutes after removing from freezer. Watch carefully and remove when it is browned. Bake the second time directly on oven rack, do not use a cookie sheet.

Jane Sebade

STRAWBERRY BUTTER FOR FRENCH TOAST

2 sticks unsalted butter

Honey to taste

8-10 medium strawberries, hulled and sliced

Put slightly softened butter in blender or food processor and process until smooth. Add 3 Tbsp. honey and blend. Continue to add honey, 1 Tbsp. at a time to taste. Add strawberries and process a few seconds until blended. Should be made soon before serving for best freshness and taste.

Kathy Hustead

STUFFED FRENCH TOAST

1 8-oz. pkg. cream cheese, softened
1 tsp. vanilla
½ c. chopped walnuts
1 16-oz. loaf French bread
4 eggs
1 c. whipping cream
½ tsp. vanilla
½ tsp. ground nutmeg
1 12-oz. jar (1½ c.) apricot preserves
½ c. orange juice

Beat together cream cheese and 1 tsp. vanilla until fluffy. Stir in nuts. Set aside. Cut bread into ten to twelve 1½-inch slices. Cut a pocket in the top of each. Fill each with 1½ Tbsp. cheese mixture. Beat together eggs, whipping cream, remaining ½ tsp. vanilla and nutmeg. Using tongs, dip the filled bread slices in egg mixture. Be careful not to squeeze out the filling. Cook on a lightly greased griddle until both sides are golden brown. To keep cooked slices hot for serving, place them on a baking sheet in a warm oven. Meanwhile, heat together preserves and juice. To serve, drizzle apricot mixture over hot French toast. Makes 10-12 stuffed slices.

Kathy Hustead

JUDY'S BEST LEFSE

3 c. boiling water
3 c. Martha Gooch instant potatoes
½ c. melted butter
3 Tbsp. cream
1 tsp. salt
1 Tbsp. sugar
1½ c. flour

Boil water. Remove from heat. Add salt, sugar, cream and butter. Stir until salt and sugar are dissolved. Add instant potatoes and stir until all flakes are dissolved. Cool overnight. The next day, mix in flour with mixer. Let set ½ hour. Use ¼ cup dough for each piece of lefse. Roll out on floured pastry sheet. Bake on lefse grill until lightly browned.

Teresa Rush

AROMA OF CHRISTMAS

3 cinnamon sticks
3 bay leaves
¼ c. whole cloves

2 lemon sections
2 pieces orange peel

Simmer over low heat in 1 quart water. Mixture can simmer all day. Add water as needed.

Kim Hayes

HOMEMADE PLAY-DOUGH

1 c. flour
½ c. salt
2 tsp. cream of tartar

1 c. water
1 Tbsp. vegetable oil
Food coloring (any color)

Mix and cook over medium heat until it forms a ball. Knead while still warm. Keeps forever in a covered container.

Jon & Kelly Kirby

CAFE VIENNA

1 tsp. cinnamon
½ c. instant coffee
⅔ c. granulated sugar

⅔ c. powdered milk or
coffee creamer

Blend in blender until powdered. Use 1-2 tsp. per cup of hot water.

Marti Kjerstad

IRISH CREME

3 eggs
1 can Borden's con-
densed milk

2 Tbsp. Hershey's choco-
late syrup

Blend in blender for 3 minutes. Add:

1 c. Irish whiskey (can
use brandy or bourbon,
too)
1 Tbsp. instant coffee

1 8-oz. carton Rich's coffee
cream
¼ tsp. almond extract
1 tsp. vanilla

Blend for 7 more minutes. Keep in refrigerator. Serve over ice or with coffee for after-dinner drink.

Mildred Rush

AMARETTO COFFEE

1½ shots amaretto 6 shots coffee, hot
1 shot cognac or brandy
Mix and top with real sweetened whipped cream.

Joan Renner

PARTY PUNCH

2 pkgs. lemon-lime Kool- 1 46-oz. can pineapple
  Aid   juice
2 c. sugar   1 qt. ginger ale
2 qts. water   2 pts. lime sherbet
Mix all ingredients except sherbet. Pour over sherbet
just before serving.

Margaret Kuntz

APRICOT SLUSH

48 oz. apricot nectar   8 oz. frozen pink lemonade
48 oz. pineapple juice   1 c. vodka
8 oz. frozen orange juice 1 c. apricot brandy
Mix and put in container and freeze. Put one ice cream
scoopful into glass and fill with 7-Up.

Bernice Anderson

HOT SPICED CIDER

½ c. sugar   2 sticks cinnamon
1 tsp. whole cloves   1 gal. apple cider
1 tsp. whole allspice
Boil first 4 ingredients with 2 c. apple cider. Add to remaining apple cider and heat.

Marcia Sawvell

ORANGE SLUSH

12 oz. frozen orange juice 2 c. sugar
12 oz. frozen lemonade   2 c. vodka
11 c. water
Boil 2 c. water to dissolve sugar. Mix remaining ingredients with this and freeze, stirring often. To serve, put
¾ c. slush in a glass and add 7-up to fill glass.

Marilyn Drewitz

HOLIDAY ORANGE EGGNOG

2 6-oz. cans frozen orange   **1 qt. milk**
   juice concentrate   **1 qt. eggnog**
2 c. water

Dilute orange juice concentrate with water; add milk. Then add eggnog. May sprinkle with nutmeg. Serve chilled.

Marjorie Hustead

INDEX

CAKES & COOKIES

DESSERTS

MAIN DISHES

CONTENTS OF STANDARD CANS

Picnic equals 1¼ cups

No. 300 equals 1¾ cups

No. 1 Tall equals 2 cups

No. 303 equals 2 cups

No. 2 equals 2½ cups

No. 2½ equals 3½ cups

No. 3 equals 4 cups

No. 5 equals 7⅓ cups

No. 10 equals 13 cups

GUIDE TO WEIGHTS AND MEASURES

1 teaspoon equals 60 drops

3 teaspoons equals 1 tablespoon

2 tablespoons equals 1 fluid ounce

4 tablespoons equals ¼ cup

5⅓ tablespoons equals ⅓ cup

8 tablespoons equals ½ cup

16 tablespoons equals 1 cup

1 pound equals 16 ounces

1 cup equals ½ pint

2 cups equals 1 pint

4 cups equals 1 quart

4 quarts equals 1 gallon

8 quarts equals 1 peck

4 pecks equals 1 bushel

SHORT NAMES WE USE IN OUR RECIPES

tsp . . . . teaspoon
Tbsp . . . . tablespoon
pt . . . . pint
qt . . . . quart
gal . . . . gallon
oz . . . . ounce
lb . . . . pound
pkg . . . . package
sq . . . . square
med . . . . medium
hr . . . . hour

SUBSTITUTIONS AND EQUIVALENTS

2 tablespoons fat equals 1 ounce

1 cup fat equals ½ pound

1 pound butter equals 2 cups

1 cup hydrogenated fat plus ½ teaspoon salt equals 1 cup butter

2 cups sugar equals 1 pound

2½ cups packed brown sugar equals 1 pound

1⅓ cups packed brown sugar equals 1 cup granulated sugar

3½ cups powdered sugar equals 1 pound

4 cups sifted all-purpose flour equals 1 pound

4½ cups sifted cake flour equals 1 pound

1 ounce bitter chocolate equals 1 square

4 tablespoons cocoa plus 2 teaspoons butter equals 1 ounce bitter chocolate

1 cup egg whites equals 8 to 10 whites

1 cup egg yolks equals 12 to 14 yolks

16 marshmallows equals ¼ pound

1 tablespoon cornstarch equals 2 tablespoons flour for thickening

1 tablespoon vinegar or lemon juice plus 1 cup milk equals 1 cup sour milk

10 graham crackers equals 1 cup fine crumbs

1 cup whipping cream equals 2 cups whipped

1 cup evaporated milk equals 3 cups whipped

1 lemon equals 3 to 4 tablespoons juice

1 orange equals 6 to 8 tablespoons juice

1 cup uncooked rice equals 3 to 4 cups cooked rice

AMOUNTS FOR 50 PEOPLE

Food as Purchased   **50 Servings**

Beans, Navy ....(3 qts.) 5½ lbs.

Beef, Ground (for meatballs or loaf) ....10 lbs.

Beef Roast ....20 lbs.

Bread (1 lb. loaf).....................................5 loaves

Butter ....1 lb.

Cabbage (shredded for salad).........................10 lbs.

Chicken (creamed or for chicken pies) ....20 lbs.

Chicken (roasted) ....25 lbs.

Chicken (salad) ....20 lbs.

Coffee (1 lb. to 2½ gal. water).......................1¼ lbs.

Cream (for coffee) ....1½ pts.

Cream (whipping, to top desserts)....................¾ qt.

Fruits (drained for salad)............................6 qts.

Gravy ....3 qts.

Ham (whole) ....16 lbs.

Ham (boned, canned) ....13 lbs.

Ice Cream (bulk) ....6½ qts.

Ice Cream (brick) ....2 gal.

Lemonade ....4 c. sugar, 2 doz. lemons, 3 gal. water

Lettuce (head lettuce salad) ....12 heads

Nuts (salted) ....2½ lbs.

Pork Chops ....12-15 lbs.

Pork Roast (rib) ....16 lbs.

Potatoes (to be mashed)...............................15 lbs.

Potatoes (creamed or scalloped).....................12½ lbs.

Potato Chips ....2½ lbs.

Mayonnaise ....1 qt.

Salad Dressing (French)...............................1 qt.

Sugar (cubes for coffee) ....1 lb.

Vegetables (canned beans, beets, carrots, peas) ......10 No. 2 cans

In order that the mailing of these books may be more convenient for our patrons, we print on this page three mail in coupons which we will be pleased to honor upon receipt of $5.95 plus $2.25 handling charge for each book desired. Address all correspondence to:

WALL DRUG COOKBOOK
Wall, SD 57790

SOUTH DAKOTA RESIDENTS PLEASE AD 49¢ PER COPY
- -

Please send me _____ copies of Wall Drug Cookbook at _____ plus _____ handling per copy.
Enclosed is my check for $_____, payable to Wall Drug.
Name _____
Street _____
City _____ State _____ Zip _____

- -

Please send me _____ copies of Wall Drug Cookbook at _____ plus _____ handling per copy.
Enclosed is my check for $_____, payable to Wall Drug.
Name _____
Street _____
City _____ State _____ Zip _____

- -

Please send me _____ copies of Wall Drug Cookbook at _____ plus _____ handling per copy.
Enclosed is my check for $_____, payable to Wall Drug.
Name _____
Street _____
City _____ State _____ Zip _____

Crescent Publishing, Inc.

Telephone (507) 962-3239 Hills, Minnesota 56138

We will help your organization with a
Money Raising Project

This book has been printed by Crescent Publishing, Inc. of Hills, Minnesota. We specialize in printing cookbooks for all types of organizations which enables these organizations to raise money for their worthwhile projects.

If your organization is interested in raising money, just fill out this form and mail it to us, and we'll be happy to send you information which gives complete details about prices, covers, etc.

Send for free information today

Crescent Publishing, Inc.
Hills, Minnesota 56138

Gentlemen:
Please send free information on compiling a cookbook. The name of our organization is:

_____

_____

Please send information to:
Name _____
Address _____
City_____ State_____
Telephone_____ Zip_____

I understand that requesting this information does not obligate me in any way.